NAME, RANK AND NUMBER

NAME, RANK AND NUMBER

Robert W. Calvey

The Book Guild Ltd
Sussex, England

The Book Guild Ltd
25 High Street,
Lewes, Sussex

First published 1998
© Robert W. Calvey
Set in Times
Typesetting by Acorn Bookwork, Salisbury

Printed in Great Britain by
Bookcraft (Bath) Ltd, Avon

A catalogue record for this book is
available from the British Library

ISBN 1 85776 207 X

I wish to express my gratitude to my late brother, Alfred, for the Frontispiece, and his valuable help with this book.

Frontispiece

By Alfred Calvey.

Name rank and number they told me,
Is all that the foe need know,
When the circumstances are hopeless,
And you're no longer part of the show,

Heed not the enemy's patter,
Or inducement to rethink your cause,
Or any subtle suggestion,
That theirs is as righteous as yours,

You're fighting for freedom and justice,
And this should soften the blow,
If you fall to the enemy's armour,
'What justice?' you still want to know,

You're fighting for God, King and Country,
They told me, so let it be,
But when the last bloody battle is over,
Will they then be fighting for me.

1

In the early hours of the morning 9 September 1943, British, American, and Allied troops made the first landings at Salerno. Amongst the many regiments making up this task force was the Reconnaissance Corps. The fact that Italy had capitulated only a few hours earlier, gave us no illusions as to the efficiency of the opposing force. We had been warned before landing, we would come up against our old enemy the 'H.G.', no not the Home Guard, the Hermann Goering regiment. Our past experience in North Africa some months earlier was not easily forgotten. Memories of booby-trapped dead German soldiers, left by these callous, murderous swine, still linger.

From the moment we hit the beach, we were immediately pinned down, by heavy machine gun fire and mortar shells from both flanks. During the next two hours the situation remained extremely grim. Eventually it became apparent that the Germans were pulling back, although the accurate German artillery was taking its toll. Our own heavy artillery was now getting ashore and going immediately into action. However, a slight lull in activities allowed our mob the 46th, Reconnaissance Corps, to advance off the beach-head and to gain the comparative shelter of a small wooded area, though not without many casualties. We were able to regroup for the job we had come to do; reconnoitre. Two of our patrols moved out and later returned to confirm that Jerry had retreated from his forward position, to what was obviously a prepared line of defence some distance inland. This made sense, for the wide open ground before us rose sharply some half a mile to wooded hilly country. From this position enemy armour could sweep the entire slope and annihilate anyone trying a frontal assault. This was also apparent to our command. Word came through for us to stay put till further

1

orders. I was glad to be off that vehicle-strewn beach where some of my mates still lay, dead or badly wounded.

The invasion bridgehead had now expanded considerably and both the British and the American armoured units; artillery and troops, were already fanning out inland on both flanks of our position. All were taking a hell of a hammering from the German 88mm guns. A week later we found ourselves inland, fighting over a wide front. The hilly terrain made progress slow and although a lot of the opposition we encountered was in small pockets, mostly skirmishes with German rear guards, we awaited the confrontation we all knew must come. To keep advancing like we had been, without further casualties, could never be that easy. As we anticipated, almost three weeks later we approached the Garigliano river and resistance was stubborn.

Our first recce patrol in this sector consisting of a corporal and three troopers, all failed to return. As any further advance must be across the river, a second fully armed fighting patrol was ordered to reconnoitre the river bank for any weak spots in the German defence.

That night I was one of the ten troopers to be picked, also two N.C.O.s and our officer; this constituted the fighting unit. It was not a very favourable night for a patrol of this kind. All the troopers were weighed down with extra equipment, some carried borrowed tommy guns, also two bren guns were taken with many extra magazines for each gun. Every rifleman had two fifty-round bandoliers of .303 ammo slung around his shoulders, two bren gun magazines in his pouches, and two hand grenades. A few miles out from our own lines we had to jump over a very small waterlogged ditch, which left me almost up to my knees in slime, and needing a helping hand out. I was carrying the bren gun at the time, also six full bren gun magazines, plus one hundred rounds of .303 ammo in my bandoliers and two hand grenades, also the spare barrel for one of our bren guns. The .303 ammunition was essential as it could have been used in my rifle, or to fill any empty bren magazines.

All this weight I was carrying made it very hard going,

2

that's why I finished up in the waterlogged ditch. All this ammo I carried made me feel like a walking ammunition dump.

Further on, nearer to the river bank, we came upon small heaps of earth thrown up from the German slit trenches, now obviously vacated. We were spread out, probably 150 yards from the river, moving in a crouching position from one mound to another. A low full moon suddenly appeared from behind a bank of cloud bathing the entire area like a massive searchlight. It also clearly lit up a machine gun post about 150 yards to our left. Our officer seeing our predicament shouted out his orders, 'Close four troop at the double,' this coincided with a lethal hail of fire from the machine gun post followed by spasmodic fire from our right flank. Everyone dived for whatever cover they could find, myself behind a slit trench mound. We were caught unawares and completely pinned down, any slight movement from us brought another burst of machine gun fire. Earth and stones sprayed up by the machine guns rained down on me. It was now obvious to everybody, including Jerry, that we were completely trapped.

After minutes, which seemed like hours, I heard what was left of the patrol shouting, 'Kamerad'. I knew then that we were all in the same boat, and this patrol was also unsuccessful. I then saw German soldiers advancing on us from our rear with fixed bayonets. The corporal who had been in the slip trench behind which I was lying started to panic, I tried to pacify him but he shouted, 'I'm going to make a run for it.' The next moment he fell dead across my legs, with a bullet through the back of his head. That decided me, I crawled clear of the corporal, raised my arms and shouted 'Kamerad' along with the rest. I started to walk slowly towards the machine gun post, wondering if I would get shot or bayonetted.

About 20 yards from the bunker I heard the sound of a rifle bolt being rammed home, seconds later a shot rang out. I hit the ground instantly, and let out a blood-curdling scream as the two grenades came together in my trousers pockets, the only place I had left to carry them. I heard someone shout,

3

'Old Calvey's had it.' It was one of the troopers who had given themselves up earlier. As I rose painfully from the ground, cursing the bloody hand grenades, two Germans with fixed bayonets escorted me up to the riverbank to a concrete gun emplacement, where the remainder of our patrol stood unarmed and dejected.

A German officer who spoke good English approached and ordered us to strip to our bare uniforms, then two of his men checked our pockets. Anything that could be used as a weapon was confiscated, also any rings, watches, cigarette cases and lighters. They left us our few cigarettes which were mostly damaged. The officer then told us we could fetch in our dead and the wounded, under an armed escort. As nine of us had survived there was obviously four missing. I knew the corporal was dead.

We found the mangled body of the sergeant beside the machine gun post, his empty tommy gun at his side. He had literally been riddled in half. We came upon the trooper moaning in a slit trench, his ankle almost severed by machine gun fire. We patched his ankle up the best we could, using his field dressing, and carried him over to the dead sergeant. The corporal had not been brought in yet, we fetched the corporal and placed him with the others by the river bank. We could not find the officer, there was no trace of him. Whether he had escaped back to our own lines, or was lying concealed, dead or wounded, we never did find out. The two dead N.C.O.s, and the wounded trooper, were put in a small pontoon boat and ferried across the river. When the boat returned, we were also ferried across three at a time, with a machine gun from both banks trained on us. The two dead could have been left to be buried where they had fallen, but this would have left evidence of the conflict, which Jerry did not want. Once we were all across we formed into some kind of marching order. Supporting our wounded trooper, and under a strong armed escort we set forth into captivity. Our war was definitely over.

2

We walked for about fifteen minutes, during which time I realized, (though still in a nightmare state) I had a hand grenade in each trouser pocket, which, amazingly enough my searchers had failed to confiscate. Arousing myself from this hideous nightmarish experience, I knew these were now useless. A chance to rid myself of the grenades came when a cloud obliterated the moon, I then dropped them both with pins intact into a ditch, which ran beside the road. Half a mile further down the road brought us to an old farm with a few dilapidated outhouses at the rear. This appeared to be the Germans' forward H.Q. we were taken into one of the outhouses which was apparently used as a first-aid post.

If this was a casualty station it was not very clean; old discarded dressings overflowed from a receptacle, straw and dried mud caked the floor. A few minutes later another German came in, we presumed he was the M.O. He instructed us to lay the wounded trooper, who was now unconscious, on the floor. The poor lighting in this room came from a few small gas filled lanterns, one of which the officer asked one of us to hold so light could be directed to wherever it was needed. The officer removed the remains of the gaiter, boot, and sock and did his best under those conditions to clean and dress the injured ankle. We were all pretty sick after seeing the M.O. attend to that gory mess, what cigarettes we did have were sadly depleted by the time he had finished.

Now the trooper's foot had been temporarily attended to, he was left on the mud caked floor. The remainder of us, after a few more questions, were taken outside to a covered lorry which we boarded. Two guards sat in the back with us, we were then driven away.

It did not seem a long journey, we arrived at what we found out later had been an Italian army barracks, the name

5

of the place was Frosinone. The barracks had been taken over by the Germans to be used as a P.O.W. collection camp. Here we were ordered to strip and were searched again and after redressing, we were taken one by one before an interrogator, who appeared to be a high ranking officer. Before leaving England we had been told if taken prisoner only give name, rank, and number. Having given him these details he then amazed me by quoting the date our regiment left England, the date and place we landed in North Africa and the actions we had been engaged in while in North Africa. He looked at me for a moment, then told me the date we left for the Salerno invasion. He named the regiments who had landed with us, also the actions the various regiments had been engaged in since landing. All he wished to know from me was if the Recce Corps had their heavy armoured scout cars over in Italy yet. I knew they had, but I told him as I was in the assault troop, I had never met up with any of the scout squadrons. He appeared to believe my lie, in fact thanked me, then gave me a cigarette, and dismissed me.

After we had all been through the interrogation they gave us a drink of ersatz coffee, and a slice of bread. We were then taken along a narrow balcony to a dingy room. This contained old straw mattresses strewn on a wooden floor, which had been left by the Italian solders. We had two grubby tattered blankets handed to us and were told to kip down. We needed no second invitation, it had been a long hard day, what with one thing and another, and now another day was dawning. As dog tired as we were it still took us time before we fell asleep.

We had not been asleep long, when we all awoke scratching also to discover the mattresses were crawling with lice, and so were we. We spent the rest of that night debugging and indeed every night after that for a couple of weeks, trying to delouse ourselves. There was no delousing unit in the barracks, and we found all the other prisoners in the same boat; lousy. It was now the major preoccupation and daily ritual of all the prisoners to strip off everything, right down to our birthday suits. Morning and night, the battle was on,

6

trying to kill off as many of the horrible things as possible. We managed to get a candle from one of the Italian civilians, so we could run the naked flame up and down the seams of our underclothes.

All the P.O.W.s were allotted a meagre food ration each day. This was pooled together and the food was cooked by four British prisoners who were said to be cooks (I think crooks a better word, as they always seemed to have more than anyone else). It didn't improve matters to discover our alleged British cooks had boiled their socks and underclothes in one of the large cooking urns they made our daily soup in. These urns were never cleaned out properly, consequently one day on top of our watery soup apart from the small pieces of cabbage there were dead lice. We scraped off as many as we could wasting the minimum of soup then scoffed the remainder as this was all the food we would be getting till the next night. What else could we have done?

Apart from the usual ration of watery carrot, or cabbage soup, we were allocated one small brown military loaf between six men each day. Sometimes we had an issue of very bitter cheese, or maybe a sickly sweet jam, which left a horrible tang in our mouth. If, I said if, these two came up at the same time mixing them together, made them almost palatable, otherwise the ersatz coffee helped to wash the so-called jam taste away.

Amongst a new batch of prisoners who arrived two days later, was a little London chap who had been living with the partisans. He spoke Italian reasonably well and his appearance was that of a typical Italian. He told me of his recapture. It appears he was in a bistro which was frequented by the Germans. As he was leaving a German officer said in a Cockney accent, 'Shut the door mate when you go out,' he closed the door then realized his mistake. He told me if he could get out of the camp somehow and make contact with a certain person who lived in Frosinone, the partisans would get him away okay (he gave me no names or any other details). He asked me if I could help in his escape bid, so we made plans to create a diversion in the dining room early that night. The best way to attract all the guards would be a fight between two British prisoners, that's one thing old Jerry did like to see. One or two other prisoners were approached clandestinely, and one agreed to the plan. My fellow prisoner and myself faked a good scrap.

The other prisoners had been previously briefed and were shouting and spurring us on, making it more realistic. This diversion had to last for at least fifteen minutes. Almost all the action took place under the dining room tables and wooden benches, thus making all the hitting and struggling a sham, but there was blood flowing freely from my nose, I'd hit it by accident on a table leg. This was the first time I had played this deceiving game, and it was a great success.

Christmas 1943 arrived, our rations never improved over this period, and the few extra hard-tack biscuits which were doled out to us could not quell our persistent hunger. To celebrate this festive season, as a treat, the Germans gave us each about a half a litre of wine, which they had most probably pinched off the Italians. The gift of three cigarettes to each prisoner was much appreciated. We know all our guards had a whip-round to supply these cigarettes, which we thought was a very kind gesture. These little comforts although meagre did help, it is said, 'beggars can't be choosers,' for that was all we were now.

The allies were getting closer day by day, and the area was being shelled or bombed frequently. Frosinone had only one vulnerable target as far as I could tell, that was a small road bridge over a river, on which the majority of German reinforcements would pass, this seemed to be the target the allies were aiming for. One bombing attack eventually succeeded in partly demolishing the bridge and cratering a large length of road. Lucky for us our camp was not hit, although some bombs dropped too close for comfort. We knew it was against the Geneva Convention, (the international agreement formulated in Geneva in 1864, establishing a code for wartime treatment of sick or wounded but revised to cover maritime warfare and prisoners of war) but the cheeky Germans had the audacity to ask us P.O.W.s for help to repair the damage.

As any help could be destructive as well as constructive, I volunteered along with the others. Any break from prison camp routine was worth having, also a chance to escape. Any opportunity like this could not be overlooked.

When we arrived on the scene, we found along with other damage the water main had been fractured. One of our guards noticed a small concave object, which he thought was a piece of the original water pipe. He thought it would fit into the broken pipe and stop the cement falling through while it was being repaired. He had no idea at all what he was doing, but he made a gesture to me to hand it to him. I soon dropped it when I noticed a small tuft of human hair on one side of it.

After two days, and a constant series of breakdowns with cement mixers, and other inexplicable disasters, our services were dispensed with, and we were confined to camp. We spent a lot of our time debugging, and were now free of the lice, the bloody little parasites. The Germans must have made some quick repairs to the road, also to the bridge, as a day or two later the entire camp was bundled into a fleet of lorries and driven across it, en route to a larger camp. The allies were obviously getting too close for Jerry's liking.

3

This new camp known as Fara in Sabina, stood completely isolated amid open fields. The camp itself was large holding about 800 to 900 prisoners with a capacity for many more. Most of the inmates were British, with about 100 American and colonial prisoners. It was completely surrounded by high double rows of barbed wire fencing, with lookout towers at vantage points, e.g. each corner of the camp. These housed two guards, a machine gun, and searchlights. There were sixteen long wooden huts in the compound to accommodate the prisoners, and on the other side of the wire was the guards' quarters, and the camp commandant's office. Our hut was right at the top end of the compound facing the wire, all the remaining huts were to our right. Although having to look through barbed wire, we had the best view of the surrounding countryside.

The food was similar to the previous camp, only this time the German cooks prepared it, and there was one added novel feature: after all the prisoners had been served, any remaining soup left in the cook's cauldron would be left outside the cookhouse, and could be had for the fastest and the strongest, at the cook's shout of 'Buckshees,' the resultant a scrimmage resembling a rugby match. Nevertheless the next day I was tempted to try my hand in this game. I handed my mate my soup and with a spare mess tin I waited the cooks shout of buckshees, as I heard 'buck' I made one mad dash I reached the cauldron, dipped my mess tin in and was smothered by a mass of arms and bodies. My mess tin fell to the bottom of the soup, and by the time the scrum had subsided I was left with an empty mess tin and bruised arm. I decided on health grounds not to attempt to play that game again.

From the doorway of our hut, we could see a donkey tethered in a field about 150 yards away. A day or two later a lone plane passed overhead and dropped a single bomb. The blast from which shook our hut, and sent a piece of shrapnel whirling through the window, and also deposited the donkey 30 yards nearer the camp, very dead. An hour or two later we noticed four P.O.W.s, accompanied by a guard loading the carcass on a handcart, they then disappeared out of view, apparently they had gone to bury it. We had forgotten the event until we found small pieces of meat in our carrot watered soup a few days later, we knew what had happened to old Neddy.

An incident then happened that impressed my young mind, (I was 21 years old, two months previous) on the changing values of society. An old soldier from our hut had been caught stealing a piece of bread from one of the other prisoners, a sordid but petty offence in civvy street, but a very serious crime in a prison camp. A court of enquiry was held by our camp leader as to the offender's fate. The choice of running the gauntlet between 80 enraged men, or taking on a certain Tich, a lightweight boxing champion of his ship prior to his capture. The old soldier opted for Tich, knowing he would not survive trying to run the gauntlet, so a ring was formed by the offended hut members.

The culprit entered the ring but made no attempt to defend himself, with his hands hanging limp by his sides, he stood in a drooping attitude, his head bent in shame, he just stared at his feet. Tich seemed reluctant to throw a punch, saying 'I can't hit a chap who refuses to defend himself,' but constant goading spurred him into action. In only a few minutes the old soldier was unconscious at his assailant's feet, and in a sorry state, a broken nose, both eyes closed, and his missing front teeth had been driven through his lips. A pitiful sight, yet the men forming the ring wanted further punishment inflicted. They thought the punishment too lenient for such a crime. The camp leader, however, stepped in, saying 'That's enough!' and detailed two chaps to drag the old soldier over to the German M.O.'s hut for treatment. From that day on, while he was in that camp, his life was hell, being assigned to all the filthiest of chores indefinitely, latrine cleaning etc.

11

About half a mile or so from the camp and hidden by tall coniferous trees, was our neighbour, a medium-sized farm. The Germans wanted one of the large barns cleared out, so a half-track vehicle could be parked undetected. I was invited to join the working party, which I did with the prospects of scrounging some extra food in the vicinity. There were four of us on the working party, accompanied by a guard. Apart from the few mentioned trees, the open terrain would have made escaping a ludicrous act. If I had been in civvies I may have taken a chance as there were many Italian farm labourers in the vicinity. The barn was full of old farm equipment and wood, this two day job we decided would last us a week. As the more agile of the four, it was agreed I should slope off on the scrounge for food every opportunity I had, the other three would cover for me.

My first recce showed that while operating as a farm, it also contained a small airstrip from which reconnaissance planes operated, a pilot's quarters, and a cookhouse. Near the barn we were to empty was a large pigsty, to which the cook made frequent visits with his swill bucket. Pushing my way past the old sow, my investigations revealed a long wide shelf, on which was an assortment of food in various stages of decay, mainly brown army surplus loaves. I snatched a loaf, broke off the mould, and tasted it, it was edible. I was in the process of stuffing another loaf in my battledress jacket, when a cold English voice commanded me to come out of the pigsty, with my hands on my head.

Obeying the order I stepped outside, and found myself facing a young German officer with a Mauser pistol in his hand, 'Why are you in there stealing pig food?' he demanded.

I hesitated, then shrugged my shoulders, then replied sheepishly, 'I'm hungry.'

'Come with me,' and he prodded me in the back with the pistol, as we walked towards our guard. I walked a little way in front of him, thinking different things, was I to be taken off the job? or taken off to be shot? Our guard sprang to attention at our arrival and received an ice cold dressing down, for his lackadaisical manner while on duty.

The officer then turned to the four of us, and in a calm, friendlier voice, said, 'I have given orders to your guard, that while you are working here, you can have any food which is available from the cookhouse after thirteen forty-five hours each day. The cook will also be notified as to these arrangements.' The officer turned and left, we were left with an irate guard on our hands.

However, his attitude softened after a visit or two down to the cookhouse, where he could have a sly smoke and a cup of coffee. We had all eaten well, as the food was the best in quality and quantity we had tasted for months. The cook apparently had known the pains of hunger and showed a soft spot by allowing us to take any leftover food back to the camp. We had to be careful accepting this offer; food was one commodity no P.O.W. would refuse. Getting it back into camp would need strategy. Although in a few months we had become experts in cheating gate guards. We were sorry when the job ended but before it did a sour note crept in. Two German airmen came to complain violently to the cook, about P.O.W.s eating their food. The cook offered them bread and cheese, we had dined on meatballs and potatoes, topped with rich thick gravy, which elevated the quarrel, an officer who had just left, must have heard the commotion and returned to intervene. His verdict was they had been given ample time to have their meals, therefore they must take pot luck.

The last morning on the job was bitterly cold, with just my battle dress on I stood shivering, my hands in my pockets for warmth. The same officer who had quelled the cookhouse dispute came past and noticed me. He then took our guard away for a few minutes, on the guard's return he handed me an almost new Italian army overcoat, and indicated it was now mine. I never did get a chance to say thank you to that officer for the coat as we never met him again. I had thanked the guard earlier, but his English was limited. At least I had met one decent German officer.

4

I had been in this camp about three weeks, then one morning after roll call the entire camp was assembled and marched out, a heavy guard escorted us to a nearby railway siding. Waiting for us was a train with a number of gloomy looking cattle trucks in the rear. We were jostled 45 at a time into each truck, the sliding doors were bolted and sealed each side, with closely nailed lengths of barbed wire fixed around the outside of the very small window. The thought of escaping was on everyone's mind, but the over-eager idiotic fools in the next truck to ours could not wait. They started ripping the floor boards up before the train had left the siding. Consequently all 45 occupants were transferred to our truck, making it almost impossible to move about. Apart from the straw strewn floor, two compressed waterproof cardboard latrines had been placed by the door, for emergency use only. Among the chaps in the truck were some long-term prisoners, released by the Italians when they capitulated, only to be recaptured by the Germans. Some had lived with the Italians and had taught themselves to speak Italian. Just the sort of chap to have with you on an escape bid.

Attempts were made to force the door open, others tried to remove boards off the side of the truck, some even started on the floor, but the overcrowding made this attempt useless. Someone produced a pack of cards, so a solo school started, but the card game became boring, so two or three of us started another escape bid on the door.

Suddenly there was a violent explosion, the train came to a shuddering halt, throwing us higgledy-piggledy to the floor. We had just disentangled ourselves when another ear shattering explosion rocked our truck on its tracks, rendering us helpless again back on the floor. Shrapnel had torn a jagged hole in the roof, and the blast had ripped one door completely off. Coming to my senses, and through the smoke and choking straw dust and other debris, I saw daylight filtering through the doorway.

Untangling myself from a heap of bodies, I made for the door without hesitation, others were desperately pushing from behind. I just managed to save myself being pushed out into a sheer drop of some 150 feet. We were perched perilously on a viaduct, most of which had been demolished. The train and four or five trucks lay embedded at the bottom of the valley, with other trucks hanging and still linked together. Our truck was balancing precariously on the very edge, and could have gone over at any minute.

It was a ghastly unbelievable sight. The only safe way to escape lay five or six trucks back along the remaining viaduct. My hands grabbed impatiently at the barbed wire reinforcing, luckily missing the vicious sharp points, but glad of its presence. I went hand over hand along the outside of the trucks, until I reached a safe place to jump down. The rear end of the train had been untouched by the bombing, therefore the occupants were still sealed up inside, trying to release themselves. I could not be concerned with their plight, my only ambition was to get as far away from the scene as soon as possible. As I scrambled breathlessly up a steep grassy slope, I heard German guards shouting, then a machine gun opened fire, sending bullets whistling dangerously close. This proved other prisoners had survived the horrific bombing, and had also escaped.

On reaching the top of the incline, I rolled over the top out of sight of the railway below. My mouth was dry, and I felt sick mostly from shock. I laid there panting and fighting to regain my breath. My thoughts were, *if you want me Jerry, come and get me.*

The other side of the hill sloped down to a small clump of bushes, I made them my next objective. I squeezed through the bramble bushes, and started creeping through the undergrowth, I was suddenly transfixed by the sound of English voices ahead of me. Stealthily I forced my way forward into a small clearing, I came face to face with two other escapees

15

from the wrecked train. They looked at me in astonishment, one of the chaps had been captured with me, on that fatal patrol, his name was Gibson.

The other chap was a stranger to me, he spoke with a Tyneside accent, he didn't seem to be put out when I called him Geordie, so that's the name he was stuck with (Gibson and Geordie had known each other in civvy street). Geordie was a little older than Gibson and me, and had been originally captured in North Africa by the Italians.

Like me, they were both pretty well exhausted, so we moved to the most dense area of our hiding place and sat down, after a short rest we discussed our next move. We knew the Germans would take a roll call of the dead, the injured, and the remaining prisoners, then start a full scale search of the area. Our final decision was to move south, in the hope of meeting up with the advancing Allied troops.

It was midwinter, the weather varied between cold and mild spells, although most of the foliage had fallen, there was still enough to give us some cover. We broke the cover of the bushes, and moved in a southerly direction using whatever concealment we could find. Eventually our cover petered out onto open ground, but luckily we came to a small farm. Geordie could speak good Italian, so he was our interpreter and spokesman. Both Gibson and Geordie had dark hair and dark complexions, and would pass as Italians easily. My complexion was completely the opposite, light skin, and very fair hair, I found an old flat cap and by wearing that, at least my hair problem was solved.

As we approached the farm a dog started to bark, a minute or two later the farmer appeared, he somehow obviously knew who we were, but was quite friendly. Geordie asked him our whereabouts, he told us we were just north of Orvieto, and warned us not to go into the town, as it was occupied by German troops. Geordie thanked him and we continued on our way southwards, making a detour to miss the town, and avoiding roads as much as possible. We travelled mostly across open muddy country, making it a laborious journey and impeding our progress, although by the late evening we must have walked seven miles. Tired and exhausted, at the next farmhouse we came to, Geordie asked if we could sleep in the barn for the night. The farmer allowed us into his house and gave us an evening meal, then apologizing said, 'Sorry you must sleep outside in the barn, it's a safeguard in case the Fascists call, as they do sometimes.' If we were discovered outside, he could claim ignorance of our presence, which would perhaps save his farm from being burnt down. This was just one of the ways the Fascists used to punish anyone helping prisoners to escape. So we spent that night in the barn with the oxen.

The farmer woke us early next morning and gave us a cheese sandwich, he also allowed us to swap our tunics and trousers for some very old civilian clothes. It was quite obvious to us although friendly, he wanted us off his property as soon as possible. Now dressed as civilians we headed south all that day, managing to get food at various places, one woman gave us some fried eggs cooked in olive oil, they tasted very greasy but were soon scoffed down, and well appreciated. Later that day at another farmhouse, we were taken into the house, a place was set for us at the table. We sat with the farmer, his wife, and their two children, the woman served us a macaroni dish, followed by a very palatable wine. That enjoyable meal kept us going for the rest of the day, right up to nightfall.

We found another barn in which to sleep that night, but first we asked the owner's permission. Before sleeping we debated whether to change our plans, and try to get to Switzerland, but eventually decided to keep our original plan. Our next day's march was uneventful, although we did encounter some German soldiers, Geordie said good morning to them in Italian, as they passed us, giving them the impression we were local farm labourers. We ended up that night in the inevitable barn, this time without the owner's permission.

Next morning at first light we were up for an early start, as I was swilling my face over from a rain butt, through a slit in the wooden wall, I noticed about ten men all armed and heading towards us. Without waiting to find out who they were, or what they wanted, we slipped out the back of the barn. Quite conveniently a ditch ran just behind the barn, this we used as cover to effect our escape, then using the shelter of a hedge, we put as much distance as possible between them and us.

Although mud caked our boots making it heavy going, we never stopped till we were out of sight. I then found I had left my army identification tags hanging on a nail in the barn. I was not going to go back for them, that was for sure (I had never taken them off before, while I was on the run).

Through making this quick getaway we had no alternative, but to travel in the opposite direction of our original journey. So we made new plans. Our plan now was to find a good hiding place, then hold up and let the allied advancing troops overtake us. We left the cover of a hedgerow, and travelled down a narrow tree-lined gravelled road.

Suddenly we were almost run down by a red sports car, which shot out of a concealed road. Gibson could not stop himself, and yelled, 'You bloody fool!' The car stopped with the screech of tyres skidding on the loose gravel, then reversed back to where we stood. The driver was a young girl escorted by a male companion. She spoke in Italian then realized we were British, apologized in English, which she told us she had been taught while at grammar school.

She got out of the car and walked towards us saying, 'My mother would probably like to meet you, and if you care to follow me, you will be introduced to her.'

We looked at each other hesitantly then finally agreed, whereupon she led us through some tall wrought iron gates, into the concealed road, then up another short drive to a small lodge. As we watchfully approached the lodge, still expecting this a trap, a man immaculately dressed opened a small side door. The girl spoke to him for a few minutes then told us to go with him, she left, returned to the car, and by the sound, drove hastily away. Leaving the three of us still deeply in thought, as we followed the manservant into what seemed a well stocked kitchen.

The man smiled then said, 'Can any of you speak Italian?'

we replied with a hand moving gesture, as much to say no. He turned, picked up a telephone, pressed a button and started speaking to someone. Geordie whispered 'He's rang the main house,' a few minutes later we heard a car approaching from that direction. We felt very uneasy, and thought we had been duped into a trap.

Some few minutes later a well dressed woman, in her early fifties, came through the lodge door greeting us in English. She told us the young lady whom we had met, was her step-daughter. From the 'phone call she had gathered we were escaped prisoners of war, and had brought us food, realizing we must be very hungry. We talked for a time, then excusing herself she left, saying 'I will come back shortly.'

Her car drove away, leaving us now more uncertain of our safety than before. The food was excellent, home cured ham with salad, white bread and butter, also plenty of tea. Trap or no trap, we scoffed the food appreciatively, what little was left was made up into sandwiches to take with us. The lodge keeper admitted he spoke English, and in our conversation told us the lady was a Contessa, and that other prisoners have been treated in a similar manner.

Taking this with a pinch of salt, we were still uncertain of the Contessa, had she been in touch with the military, were they outside waiting? The Contessa returned and we resumed our conversation, during which she let slip she was a Contessa. As the conversation continued we found we could trust our host, then thanking her for her hospitality, we decided to leave, (as Geordie said,) 'While the going's good.'

The Contessa placed a kindly hand on my shoulder as I approached the door, then from her handbag she handed each of us a packet of twenty cigarettes and 200 lira, then wished us all good luck on our travels. As we were just about to leave she asked for our home addresses in England, as she would like to write to us after the war was over. We granted her this request, and accepted her explanation as to the reason why we could not have her name and address. If found on us, should we be recaptured it would jeopardize her and any other escaping prisoners who should be unfortunate

19

enough to be her temporary guest.

We left the lodge and carried on in our original direction, we mulled over various ideas and opinions as to our future strategy. One idea was to buy train tickets and travel south, this sounded brilliant at the time. Our plans were cut short by the sight of German soldiers marching towards us, in an open formation, about a quarter of a mile away, this we took for a search party. We cut across the fields to a hedge, using this as cover and travelling its length, we gained the shelter of a small spinney. Sitting on a fallen tree we pondered over our predicament. Many ideas were suggested but none more appropriate than our plan to hold up somewhere, this would avoid the constant fear of detection.

With this plan now paramount, we left the spinney travelling cross country till nightfall, meeting nobody, completely lost in a muddy patchwork of fields. We were all very tired and desperate; we kept on searching for somewhere to sleep. Tucked away in the corner of a field we found an old tractor covered with tarpaulin, rigging this into a rough tent, we ate the last of our sandwiches and tried to sleep, all huddled together to try and keep warm.

It had been a sleepless night for all, by morning we were glad to be on the move again, to help get our circulation going to thaw out our frozen limbs. After a few miles travelling we reached a small village, which was deserted at that early hour, apart from four nuns we met at the outskirts. Geordie said good morning to them, then we found one of them could speak English. We chatted to them for some time, they told us the Germans had passed through that village yesterday moving south. We never asked if they were a mechanized unit, if they had been, they would be well out of the area by now. Thus making our southward journey a little easier.

Before going on their way, the nuns gave us each a heart shaped embroidered linen prayer pouch, (which I still possess) containing a folded prayer sheet. Alas, my prayer sheet was stolen.

The village seemed to burst into activity suddenly, as the nuns blessed each of us, before resuming their journey. We

20

entered the village and feeling thirsty we tried knocking on a few doors, with the hope of getting a glass of water. One decrepit woman gave us a glass of wine which was the worst we had ever tasted. However, Geordie thanked her for us and we moved further into the village. We knocked on several other doors in our quest for water, but received vino instead.

Eventually we did get a glass of water from a young mother with a howling baby in her arms. We were astonished to see the mother give the infant, barely three months old, two large spoonfuls of a potent wine to placate it, which it did immediately. We marvelled at the child's calmness, as we left the village.

5

By late afternoon we had travelled a fair distance, and were passing through an area comprising of small scattered hamlets and villages. With no sleep the previous night and our food supply finished, we were both physically and mentally exhausted, and in bad need of sustenance. We tried several houses in the various villages for food and a place to sleep, only to be met with point-blank refusal every time, the same reason being given, the Fascist patrols were active in the area. This in itself should have warned us away from the district, but we were too tired, hungry, cold and weary to think of safety. We had just reached the outskirts of a village when we slumped on a grass verge and debated our plight. I had noticed a small bistro in the main street of the village, while we sat resting, I mentioned this to the others. Considering the pitfalls, we decided we would return and check it out, attempting to get food and lodgings for the night, regardless of expense. At all the houses we had previously called upon, requesting food, we received the same answer. '*Mangiare? niente, Tedeschi prendere, Tedeschi prendere tutti.*' This was a falsehood, there seemed to be an abundance of food all about this area.

We retraced our steps, agreeing Geordie should do all the talking, we entered the bistro. Inside the light was very poor, tobacco smoke filled the room, about a dozen or so customers were sitting around, some in animated discussion. We found an empty table, I dropped my Italian cigarettes and matches on top as a guise, Geordie then ordered vino for three, which seemed was the only refreshment they sold.

A man sitting at a nearby table nodded and said, '*Buona sera*,' Geordie replied, then beckoned him over to our table. He pulled his chair round and sat beside us and entered into conversation, speaking Italian. In a desperate bid to achieve our means, we hinted we were escaped army officers. Geordie spoke to him for a minute or two then told us, the newcomer could speak English, whereupon the man bent forward and in a whispered speech said, 'Be very careful who you speak to in here. I advise you to drink up and leave, this place is a hang out for the local Fascist group,' and finishing his own drink, added, 'If you wait till I've been to the toilet, I'll come with you, I can help you.'

He got up and made his way to a small door beside the bar, and disappeared from view. Gibson and Geordie soon swallowed their drinks, 'I'm not all that fond of vino, so I left some of mine. We sat there and waited patiently. He was gone a long time, so long in fact that in my tired mind I sensed something was wrong. Quietly I said to the others, 'He's taking a blinking long time to have that pee, let's get out of here, I don't trust that geezer.'

We got up and moved casually to the door and out onto the street, and stopped dead. Strung out across the road at both ends of the village, about 150 yards apart, was a line of armed men and youths. We looked up and down the road, estimating the furthest line to us, we decided to turn right. As we walked as slowly as we could, the two lines started closing in towards us from both directions, at approximately the same pace as us. Within a very few seconds, the bistro door behind us opened and our English speaking friend, of a few minutes ago stood there with a half a dozen cronies. My mind worked overtime thinking of a way out of this situation, when I noticed a stone wall about five foot high. Nothing was said, but we threw ourselves over the wall as one man, and scrambled off into a small field of rough pasture. Tired as we were, but with fortitude, we ran like hell. The distant barking of dogs indicated there was no hesitation by them to release the vicious hounds which accompanied the armed men. If only we had the men to deal with, we stood a good fighting chance of avoiding capture, the dogs were a different kettle of fish altogether, they were gaining on us at a great rate.

In the corner of the field was a mountain of house bricks, and we headed for them in a last desperate attempt to rid ourselves of the yapping dogs, who were now only a few yards away from us. Children had been playing with the bricks, and had built some play houses. We were exhausted, and could not run any more, we dived one by one into the nearest play hut, blocking the entrance from inside with loose bricks. The dogs had found our lair, some of the dogs pranced about outside, creating a bedlam of noise, while the majority laid snarling at the blocked entrance. All of us were panting heavily fighting to regain our breath, and completely helpless. It was certainly only a matter of minutes before our so-called Italian friend, along with his henchmen, would arrive to administer the *coup de grace.*

Approximately five minutes in fact. He was apparently the leader of this Fascist group, as we could hear him laying down the law to his subordinates.

He addressed us in English, 'You have exactly ten seconds to come out and surrender, or my men have orders to shoot you where you are.' We waited shivering, as much from fright, as from the cold, could he just be bluffing? As he started to count, rifle barrels poked their noses through the gaps between the bricks. We hoped he would stop his count, and wait until cold or hunger drove us out. Further resistance was useless, and at the count of eight, we shouted, *'Okay call off the dogs'.* The dogs were rounded up and leashed, and the rifles were withdrawn from our hideout.

After clearing the bricks from the doorway we crawled out, depressed and tired, we could hardly get to our feet, while the surly, motley crowd of Fascists, (some were only about 12 to 14 years old) surrounded the three of us. We were quickly frisked, and relieved of what little possessions we had, i.e. our money and cigarettes, and then led back to the village, with 14 heavily armed guards around us. They must have thought we were very important prisoners (two troopers and a private). As we approached the outskirts of the village the leader brought us to a halt, then dismissed all the guards except one lad of about fourteen, who lovingly cradled a sub-machine gun in his arms. He was hoping one of us would try and make a run for it, as he seemed itching to use it, but we

24

spoilt his pleasure.

We stood side by side on the roadway, the leader walked up and down looking at us for a minute or so, then told me to remove my Italian army overcoat. I started to slip the coat off my shoulders, as I did so, the lad behind prodded me in the back with his gun, and said something in Italian. I continued to remove my coat and received a louder warning, also a much harder jab from his gun.

'What's that silly bastard behind me saying?' I asked Geordie, with my coat halfway off.

'He's telling you to keep your coat on, or he will shoot you,' replied Geordie, so I put it back on, whereupon, the leader came striding up to me and slapped my face.

'I told you to take that coat off, how dare you disobey me,' he shouted, as his temper, also his gun filled hand rose to deliver another blow to my face or head.

I replied harshly, 'Supposing you tell that presumptuous bastard school-kid behind me what you want me to do.'

My reply irritated the Fascist leader, he spoke sharply to the lad in his native tongue, then turned back to me. 'Now take that bloody coat off,' which I did, without any reaction from baby-face.

The leader conferred with the lad quietly for a while, then said, 'You are wearing civilian clothes and cannot identify yourselves, therefore you are spies, and will be shot.'

'What about Gibson's, and my army pay books?' I asked, and he shrugged,

'You could have picked them up anywhere,' as much to say, there are lots of British army pay books lying around in Italy.

A high wall with a slope leading up to it, partially circled the village, he ordered us to climb the short grassy slope, and stand with our backs against the wall at the top. The gun crazy lad took up a position some thirty yards below, and trained his tommy gun on us. Our execution now seemed imminent, I stood between Gibson and Geordie. As I looked down I noticed a shallow ditch overgrown with weeds and tall grass, not visible from the road.

Instantly a foolhardy idea sprang into my mind, to feign death at the first round fired. In a situation like this, one's mind plays queer tricks. I decided to roll down the slope and fall into the ditch, from there make a last desperate effort to relieve the gun from the lad, if I have to be shot, it's better to go down fighting.

Reprieve however, came in a different form. A priest walking along the now moonlit road, approached the two below us, he spoke to them for some length of time, then crossed himself and walked slowly back towards the village. A minute or two later we were ordered to come back down onto the road. We did that with alacrity, and a sigh of relief, we looked at the two Italians as to say, that's one up to us so far. The priest apparently held more sway in the village than the Fascist movement.

Once more we stood in the roadway contemplating our destiny, we were told we would spend a night in a civilian prison, and be closely questioned in the morning. As we moved off to face the music, the double-crossing swine was in front, and trigger happy schoolboy positioned himself behind us, still hoping we would do something foolish, so he would have a good excuse to squeeze the trigger. We were led further into the village. The prison was of medium size, stone built, and close to the fateful bistro, we must have passed it in our escape bid. On our arrival we were bundled into a tiny cell that already housed three other prisoners of war, who also wore civilian clothing.

The cell was no larger than nine foot by six foot, and most of that area was taken up by a large table. This in itself measured some six feet by four feet, restricting our movements considerably. I found out the other P.O.W.s had been captured in North Africa, and had been in an Italian prison camp until released on Italy's capitulation, they had just been recaptured in this very village. The cell floor was stone and too cold and wet to sleep on, so all six of us ended up sitting on the table, dangling our legs over the sides, unable to sleep, and extremely cold.

At early dawn we heard the key grate in the lock, and a

bolt being withdrawn, our bistro friend had returned with six armed cronies. After being pushed through the cell door, almost two at a time, we were forcefully manhandled, and jabbed with gun butts, along a short corridor, then pushed through an open doorway, into a brightly lit room. We were glad to get out of that cell; apart from the damp, cold, cramped conditions, the cell smelt vile. After 48 hours without sleep and very little food, I felt like a zombie, and imagined Gibson and Geordie felt the same.

A tubby superintendent wearing rimless spectacles, sat at a desk fingering a beige folder, then commenced questioning our three cell mates first. Before he had time to get a reply to his first question, our big-headed shifty bistro friend, interrupted forcefully, wanting to know where they had obtained their civilian clothes. They told him from a farmer, in exchange for a quantity of cigarettes and money. They were then asked for the farm's location, they replied, 'On a hillside about three miles away.' The three of them were taken out on to the roadway to indicate the direction of the farm, but why us three had to go out, and for what reason or purpose, we never did know, there were ample guards to keep us covered.

Outside, one of the three pointed to a white house, which could just be seen way up on a hillside, amongst a clump of tall coniferous trees. When we had all filed back into the room, the same questions were levelled at us. Geordie and Gibson told him they had stolen their civvy clothes from a farmhouse about thirty miles away, but were hazy about direction, as we had made so many detours.

He turned on me angrily, (he must have had it in for me over the coat dispute, from yesterday,) wanting to know how I became the owner of an Italian army overcoat, which surprisingly was still in my possession. I told him a German officer had given the coat to me just after I had been captured, and as for my civvy rags, I had swapped my British uniform with a scarecrow soon after escaping. His look was one of disapproval. My coat was unbuttoned and for a while he eyed me up and down. Eventually, he seemed satisfied with my story. (My civilian attire was typical scarecrow wear, the trousers and jacket resembled a patchwork of grey, it was almost impossible to determine the original colour.)

He asked a few more questions, mostly about the various P.O.W. camps we had been interned in, paying more attention to our last camp. On completion of his questions, which, we must have answered to his satisfaction, the six of us were taken outside into a small courtyard, and given a piece of bread and a portion of cheese each. Our first food the three of us had eaten for approximately twenty hours. As we gobbled this down, the superintendent, accompanied by the skunk, told us the German authority had advised him to get us ready to be transferred to one of their prison camps. We waited in the courtyard which was heavily guarded, any escape attempt was out of the question, but our minds never rejected the subject.

6

We all gave a sigh of relief, when about a quarter of an hour later a German lorry drew up outside the archway which led into the courtyard. Alighting from the vehicle first was an officer, instantly followed by four soldiers, two armed with automatic weapons, the other two carried rifles. A fifth soldier sat in the cab with the door ajar, weighing up the situation, then decided to stay put, he slammed the door shut, and lit a cigarette.

The German officer entered the gaol then after a few minutes, he and the prison superintendent appeared still talking, we were the target of their conversation as a pointed finger indicated. The officer, who could speak only pidgin English, ordered us to get on the lorry with the four guards, who sat two at each end of the vehicle, he then jumped in beside the driver, and we drove off. It was a release from torment, all those bloody blackshirts wanted to do was shoot us. As we passed through the village, I noticed the trigger-happy schoolboy loitering outside the bistro, still toting his gun. He probably sleeps with the damned thing.

A few miles later we skirted a large hill with a farmhouse at the top burning fiercely. This was where the other P.O.W.s had obtained their civilian clothes, our Fascist friends had obviously paid them a visit.

About an hour's more driving brought the lorry to a halt, at what first appeared to be a small chalk quarry, and possibly had been at one time. An area of hillside had been cut back to produce a vertical wall of earth and chalk, some forty foot high, with a base area about seventy-five yards square. This area had been fenced in on three sides by high barbed wire, with a wide barbed wire gate in the middle of the front fence. The compound contained six moderate sized wooden huts, but no lookout towers or searchlights, it was apparently a temporary transit camp for P.O.W.s.

We were ordered off the lorry and locked inside one of the huts, inside the wooden floor was strewn with well-trodden straw. A small window too high to see through without assistance, was letting in the only light we had. The thought of escaping was at fever pitch, the door was no way out, a floorboard was removed with the intentions of going out under the hut. Our quiet hard work, and our hopes were dashed to hell, on finding, four inches underneath, hard chalky ground. Dropping the board back irrespective of noise, we sat depressed. Later we heard the sound of two other lorries arriving and prisoners talking.

Approximately one hour later we were all mustered outside for roll call; we had added another dozen prisoners to our little camp.

A middle aged bespectacled officer addressed us in fluent English, 'As you can see no doubt, this is just a temporary camp. You will stay here overnight, before being moved to another camp and eventually sent to Germany. I advise you not to attempt to escape as apart from the guards, who will shoot to kill, there are guard dogs running loose around the camp, also trained to kill. If anyone thinks of climbing that face,' he pointed to the back of the camp, 'I warn you, I have two machine guns waiting up there, and a patrol with dogs, all ordered to kill on sight.'

Apart from the bread and cheese we had eaten in the village lock-up, we had no more food all that day or night. The morning roll call found all the eighteen of us very tired, to speak for our group, and immensely hungry, a mess tin of ersatz coffee seemed to temporarily revive us. We had just finished our coffee, when ordered back onto the lorries, this time we only had two armed guards in the back with us.

7

It was early afternoon when we arrived at a large camp, the rows of dark coloured huts contained mostly British prisoners, a hundred or so other prisoners were American, and Canadian. There must have been at least 800 prisoners houses within these huts, many like us, still wearing civilian clothes, the camp was by no means full to its capacity.

It was a strongly guarded camp, two lookout towers at the entrance, each tower manned by two guards, one with a sub-machine gun, the other carried a rifle. These towers could rake the entire frontal area of the camp, and like the other towers located at each corner, housed a mounted machine gun and a searchlight. A tall twin barbed-wire fence ran all the way round except at the far end, there just the one fence stood, its twin being renewed by Italian labourers. The original fence, I was told had been destroyed by some 3,000 overjoyed prisoners, who burnt the wooden fence posts when the news broke that Italy had capitulated.

At this end of the camp, the guards were doubled day and night. The remainder of the outside wire was patrolled by two armed guards, one handled a vicious-looking guard dog. At night these guards were also doubled.

Talking to an inmate, who had been there a month, I was told the camp was near a place called Laterina, and in spite of strong security, some half a dozen escapes had occurred over the past three weeks, mainly through the fence which was now being renewed, I assumed. I informed Gibson and Geordie, about my short conversation with the older inmate, adding, *'if either of you decide to make a break, you can count me in.'*

We have taken that for granted, they replied. Although we had no intentions of trying anything until we had some food and sleep, to get over the privations of the last three days.

31

The lavatory blocks were situated roughly four foot from the lone fence, at the end of camp. The replacement of the second fence failed to materialize within the time of our occupancy. A small window inside the toilets, which we found opened noiselessly gave access to the roof. We toyed for two days with the idea of getting onto the roof then leaping over the top of the fence, which was about a foot and a half below roof height, hoping to land without breaking a leg. A rough map was made from the information gleaned from various sources, as if our escape was successful, we wanted to travel in the right direction.

We decided to wait for a wet night, when apparently the guards and their dogs stayed under shelter. Anxiety filled our waiting hours, then the next night it rained almost constantly, but Gibson backed out saying the roof would be too slippery to jump from, it would be suicidal, and he didn't fancy dangling from a barbed wire fence all night. The escape attempt was postponed for that night, which meant at least another day facing that bloody barbed wire.

Moonlight for the next two nights, made us shelve our plans temporarily. Our anxiety caused friction between us and some of the other prisoners. Our keyed up minds snapped at the least provocation.

On the third night conditions were ideal for our bid for freedom, but it was Geordie this time who complained of stomach pains, and not feeling too well, suggesting Gibson and I should try it alone. The two of us trying it would be useless, as we needed Geordie's fluent Italian to make the effort worthwhile, besides that we made a good team.

It was then agreed that if Geordie was okay the next night, we would definitely go for sure, rain or no rain. Geordie was fit by the next afternoon, but speaking to Gibson I found him rather dubious about the attempt, and I put it to him bluntly.

'*Are we going over the bloody wire or not?*'

He shrugged his shoulders and said '*Why not leave it for the time being, we can always go another night?*' and Geordie seemed to agree with him.

'Fair enough,' I told them, 'I have been ready on every

occasion to go, and you've both backed out! It's no blinking joke getting all keyed up, only to be let down by one excuse after another. If you make your minds up to have a go, good luck to you, and I hope you make it, but count me out!'

I left the two of them sitting on Gibson's bunk, as I returned to my own. We remained friendly the rest of the next day, and carried on with our usual daily routine, and by the time I kipped down for the night, I had dismissed any immediate thoughts of escape from my mind.

My bunk was down the other end of the hut, so before turning in, I popped down to say goodnight to Gibson and Geordie, adding 'see you in the morning.'

Next morning I was up early but couldn't find Gibson or Geordie anywhere, and when roll call came it was obvious they were missing.

Another prisoner said, 'I saw your mates leaving the hut early this morning, I think they have made a break for it.'

'*Yes I know,*' I replied, '*good luck to them.*'

What method they had used I could but guess. Five escapes were made that night, two escapees had walked straight through the front gates at dawn, carrying one of the large wooden fence posts. The post had been left inside the compound by mistake, one of the Italian labourers will carry the can for that. Rumours about the camp indicated that two men, waited for the new guard replacement, and told them in faultless Italian, they had been let into the compound by the previous guard, who for security reasons had locked the gates behind them. They had been ordered to retrieve the post before the prisoners were awake, to stop them using it as fire wood. Without querying the Italian's actions, the guard opened the gate, and watched the two men vanish behind a pile of posts. The two who had walked through the gates, I assume, were Geordie and Gibson.

I could understand why they did not want me with them, firstly, the post carrying only needed two men, and secondly, my fair hair and complexion was a definite disadvantage in a country of predominantly dark haired people.

In spite of all the escapes, still a large number of prisoners wore civilian clothing, rumours spread throughout the camp that British uniforms were to be issued, and all civilian clothing burnt, but nothing ever came of it.

Over the next few weeks I got back into the habitual boredom of prison life, and struck up new acquaintances, but no one came up to standard of Geordie, for enthusiasm and initiative. During the brief time I had known him, he proved to be one of the coolest companions I have ever met. Of all the escapes, in my time at Laterina, getting that fence post through the gates, was merited very highly.

The camp monotony was broken one day by the entertainment of two Yanks, who decided to murder each other, after heated words between them exploded into fury. One Yank was pushed through an open doorway, followed by his assailant, cursing and swearing.

The scrap which followed, lasted about ten minutes and was a no holds barred affair, with almost an even tally on both sides of black eyes, bloody noses and split lips. It ended in a loving embrace with both walking away arms around each other's shoulders, and the best of friends.

Another incident happened that day, a fellow inmate and myself agreed to pool our cigarette resources. I stripped every stale, evil smelling stub free of paper, and with the scrapings of fluff, and dust from my fob pocket, placed it with his scanty mixture of dry tobacco and tea leaves he had in a small tin, which once contained salt. The very few granules of salt would enhance the flavour, we hoped. We dampened the dried mixture sufficiently to make it workable, our cigarette paper was a small page from a hymn book, we had found partly burnt. We manipulated the concoction into a super-sized cigarette, or rather cigar. The second attempt to light the masterpiece was a success. I hesitated for a moment, then took my first puff, and almost coughed my lungs up. I passed it to my mate who looked at it in a quizzical way, shrugged his shoulders, and started puffing happily away, he must have had leather lungs. His happiness came to an abrupt stop, when a heavy drag ignited a hard ball of salt in the tobacco, the cigarette sputtered then flared up and exploded in his face, actually singeing his eyebrows. He spat the flaming article to the ground treading it underfoot, yelling, 'Bloody salt.'

Other escape attempts were made from time to time, some must have succeeded, or the unlucky ones were shot in the attempt, or perhaps transferred to another camp, none ever returned to Laterina. I decided to wait for our move to Germany before trying to escape, for after all, Germany was a country of predominantly fair haired people. A week later after morning roll call the entire camp was mustered in the compound and after a brief search of personal belongings, in my case nil, we were marched to a nearby railway siding. Accompanying us were heavily armed guards with ferocious looking guard dogs. We were en route for Germany.

8

It was about a half an hour's march to the sidings, and on our arrival, we found a train awaiting, identical the one I had been blown out of some few weeks earlier, only this one was definitely longer. It consisted of cattle trucks with barbed wire reinforced sides, and contained the same type of compressed cardboard latrines, also straw on the floor. Forty-five men were assigned to each truck, and as I clambered aboard visions of my last train journey flooded back, a memory I wish not to recall. I felt apprehensive of a similar trip.

My mind was soon taken off these matters by the intense cold, the weather having suddenly changed dramatically. I felt it worse because I no longer had my uniform, just thin threadbare civilian clothes, my Italian army overcoat, and socks and boots so completely worn out I was actually walking bare footed. When all the trucks held their quota of prisoners, the sliding doors were bolted and nailed up with barbed wire, as before. After a final check to make sure we were completely sealed up, most of the guards and their dogs boarded the train, the others marched off the way we had come, apparently returning to the Laterina camp. The train slowly pulled out from the cold deserted siding, leaving us wondering what life will be like in a German prison camp.

The train travelled all day, stopping occasionally at sidings to allow troop or munitions trains to pass. At one stop additional guards boarded the train, then the doors were opened and we were allowed to stretch our legs. It was a great feeling to be out into the fresh air, if it was only for a few minutes, the mess tin of coffee (ersatz) given to us was very hot and this helped to warm us slightly. There must have been fifty guards, mostly armed with sub-machine guns covering the stretch of railway line on which we had stopped, so escape was out of the question.

Before being ordered back into the trucks, most of us urinated against the trucks' wheels to save using the inside latrines, a comment was voiced from someone to the effect that they wished these wheels were the German guards.

It was early evening and freezing, some of the coffee that had been spilt was already frozen. I appreciated the fresh air but was only too glad to get back inside, away from the now freshening wind, even though inside was like a refrigerator. I plonked down in a corner, browned off to hell. I curled myself into a ball with my knees under my chin, I could not feel them.

The truck doors were bolted and resealed, and the train continued onwards, but only for a couple of miles or so before it stopped and was shunted onto a side line for the night. Sleep to me was out of the question, my feet were now so cold. I asked a well-clad Scotsman nearby to loan me his cap comforter to wrap round them. He refused, and sat there like a bundle of khaki clothing. When I repeated my request, the only answer I received was, 'Do you want me to bloody freeze to death?'

By morning all the metal parts inside the truck had half an inch coating of ice, and the wooden sections were thick with frost, which glittered in the early morning light. The train started off late that morning, from what we could gather from an overhead guard's conversation, the engine had been uncoupled during the night to move essential war supplies. We travelled non-stop till early afternoon when the doors were opened we found the ground covered with six inches of snow. Armed guards with Alsatian dogs lined the entire length of the train, which had stopped at some remote part of the track, no siding or station was visible. In the distance we could just make out a familiar sight, a square of tall lights, behind which, we knew would be a double barbed wire fence. An English voice behind a megaphone ordered us to leave the train and line up into some kind of marching order. This was our new camp, and we were obviously in Germany.

I shuffled painfully behind the others to the doorway, and dropped down to the snow covered ground. I thought for a moment I had landed on my knees, as from there downwards was completely numb. Both my feet were frostbitten. I hobbled in agony a long way back behind the others towards the camp, wondering if I would ever make it, I did eventually, with a guard to ensure I did not make a run for it. (Run? I could hardly bloody well walk). To me at that moment that prison camp seemed the most inviting place on earth. I entered the camp compound where the others stood in ragged formation, I was forced to hold on to two fellow prisoners to remain upright. As the gates slammed shut behind us a German officer, positioned himself at the centre of the square we had formed, he addressed us in English.

'You will be taken in batches to the showers, and afterwards medically examined. All civilian clothing will be burnt and uniforms issued to those without them. Those already with uniforms will have them fumigated. You will then be allocated huts according to your nationality, and given food.' His last remarks sounded like music to my ears.

9

We entered the showering room in groups of about twenty-five at a time, four armed guards counted us in and out. When my turn came, I needed assistance to get under the shower, at first it was lovely. The steaming hot water began to thaw out my frozen body, that is, except my feet, which under the hot water began swelling to an alarming size. I dried myself and was assisted into another room, where I received a decent second-hand British army uniform, a pair of wooden clogs, and two pieces of cloth about eighteen inches square, known as sock rags. My feet had swollen so much, to wear my clogs was an impossibility. The nauseating pain was so intense I could no longer stand on them, and had to be carried into the M.O.'s room.

Here I was examined for any contagious disease, and lice, I was given a clean bill of health in regards to this. I was then given two inoculations, one in my arm, another just under my right nipple, which instantly doubled me up in pain for a few minutes. All the new intake followed the same procedure, the inoculations made some men vomit, and some of the weaker prisoners fainted. On leaving the M.O.'s room, everybody was told all we new arrivals would be interrogated next morning. Ten other prisoners were assigned to the same hut as I and with their help found our allotted hut. The sock rags were the only covering I had wrapped round my feet, these fell off from time to time, and I realized my feet seemed less painful when bare, so I put the rags in my pocket.

The hut was large and contained rows of two-tiered bunks, accommodating some seventy or eighty men. The lower bunks were naturally all occupied, prisoners sat indulging in their various mannerisms. I had to be content with an upper berth, which didn't help my now bare swollen feet. On entering our hut we had each been given a Red Cross food parcel and a couple of blankets, and after being assisted on to my bunk, I had a snack from my food parcel then settled down to sleep.

This soon became impossible, the itching and burning of my feet, now so intense I was crying out in pain, and disturbing the other prisoners. Eventually one came over to my bunk to complain, but realizing my trouble, suggested I rubbed butter from my parcel over my feet, which I did, he promised to reimburse me for the butter I would use. The relief from that butter was considerable, and I eventually fell asleep. I would never have thought Maple Leaf butter had such a soothing quality.

The next morning I was woken by the same fellow who had mentioned the butter the night before, he told me he was our hut leader. He threw a tin up to me saying, 'Here's a new tin of butter I promised you last night,' then he asked about my feet, and did I think I could wear my clogs. I removed my sock rags, and gingerly tried on a clog. When he saw it was useless, he asked for two volunteers to help me get about while my feet were in this condition, and two from a nearby bunk agreed to act as Nanny.

Later these two carried me to the interrogation room, where I was expecting to be scrupulously cross-examined. All the officer wanted to know was my name, rank, and number, after writing my name on a small green card, he gave it to me, also written on the card was my prisoner of war number. He told me the card must be carried at all times as an identity card, and produced on request, failing to do so is a punishable offence. He also asked for my civilian occupation, possibly to add to their list of tradesmen available for voluntary duties. I told him I worked in the hat trade, he registered me as machine operator, actually it was the car industry. I had once worked in the ribbon trade, and knew enough about ribbons to bluff my way through any questions he may put to me. According to the answers given by the rest of the men, this officer must have thought England was a nation of layabouts and shop assistants. None admitted to any knowledge of engineering, to avoid being bribed into working in German war factories, as I found, quite a few French and Polish had.

But none of the British prisoners of war, to my knowledge were interested in any of the bribes or promises made no matter how tempting. The officer gave me a pre-printed card to send home to my parents, to notify them I was a prisoner of war, and was well. He explained all I had to do on this card was to strike out the words I did not wish to use, then repossessing the card, and the pen, after I had finished, he added, 'You will be allowed to send two letters and three postcards home each month. The cards and the special letter-cards will be allocated to you. You will not mention the camp in any way, or the weather, or other classified information, if so, your mail will not be sent.'

My helpers then ferried me to another hut, where I was fingerprinted, and photographed with my prison number hung around my neck. I felt like a convicted murderer. All this interrogation, which was apparently routine procedure, was used as a reference should any prisoner escape. Eventually I was carried back to the hut with my blanket wrapped round my feet, and only one thought in mind, to rest them. My feet and ankles were still blown up like balloons, and very painful, the swelling seemed to be increasing. I was told to report sick.

Next day I saw the German M.O. who gave me a small box of crystals, which I had to dissolve in warm water and bathe my feet in twice daily. Within a week I was hobbling slowly about under my own steam. I thanked the two fellows whose help I had depended on, and offered each a gratuity of cigarettes, but both declined the offer.

I was soon getting into the camp routine, also getting more information of what was happening in the world outside. The camp had an illicit home made wireless set, which moved from hut to hut at regular intervals, this was tuned in to one station and used for one purpose only, B.B.C. news broadcasts. Keeping this concealed from the German ferrets was a work of art, and entailed a rigid lookout system. To ensure the German propaganda did not falsify the news later, a stenographer accompanied the set to copy down all news items of importance. Within a short time of the broadcasts, duplicate copies were smuggled to each hut, to be read out to the eager

eager waiting inmates, after which the news sheets were destroyed. This system, I was told, had been operating successfully for over a year, after a planted useless wireless had been confiscated. The prisoners were almost as up to date with the progress of the war as those in England.

The camp also boasted a shop that did brisk barter trade in food items, from the Red Cross parcels, also in cigarettes. A board displayed in the doorway would announce the shop's current stock along with a price list, the major currency unit being cigarettes. I visited the shop only once, to purchase a packet of biscuits, this type of biscuit was only obtainable from the Canadian Red Cross parcel. By soaking the biscuit first then adding hot made up Klim, (powdered milk) and sugar, or raisins, made a substantial porridge. Frequent visits to the shop soon knocked a major hole in a prisoner's cigarette rations, although food from the Red Cross parcels could be sold to the shop, for cigarettes, of course the shop had another price list, the exchange rate being considerably in their favour.

I had been in this camp, Stalag IVB, about two weeks or so, and learnt only ranks below sergeants were detailed for working parties, although some sergeants wangled it to get on a working party, to break the humdrum life of prison camp. One morning just after roll call, an officer accompanied with a guard entered our hut and called for attention. 'If and when your name is called out, you will assemble outside,' he said. My name was among those called, so I collected what few items I possessed and moved outside, where eventually some two hundred prisoners from various huts assembled. Then, ten at a time we were taken into another hut, completely stripped and searched, while other guards searched our clothing. After redressing we reassembled outside. We were split into three groups and lined up, one group of about a hundred moved towards the gate while the other two groups waited. The first group was checked through the gate by file and photograph, then loaded onto a seemingly endless line of covered lorries and driven away. Our turn was next, but as I was passing through the gate, a bayonet was thrust within inches of my chest, I was pulled from the line and rescrutinized. The haggard, pained, unshaven picture I presented when the photo was taken bore but a faint likeness to my present self. The officer was, however, eventually satisfied as to my identity and I was passed through and on to a waiting lorry. I was on the move again, where to I could only guess, it's quite possible it would be a working camp. Our group comprised of sixty P.O.W.s, from all walks of life, to contemplate as to what kind of camp, would be impossible.

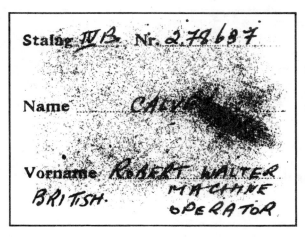

Copy of the author's prisoner of War Registration Card, issued in Stalag IVB, February 1944. This was carried at all times, as an identity card.

Counterfeit copy of the German ration card. These were dropped by the R.A.F. over the German towns and cities. With the intention of weakening the German economy.

10

We drove for several hours, occasionally stopping where the road narrowed to allow other military vehicles to pass, when at last the lorries pulled into the new camp's compound. It was a large camp and already occupied by prisoners, in this compound all British. It was a typical P.O.W. camp, surrounded by the familiar high twin barbed-wire fences, approximately ten feet apart, it also had a restraining wire, which we called a safety wire. This single strand of barbed wire, was about knee high, and if one crossed unaccompanied by a guard, or without permission, one would be instantly shot. The machine guns and searchlights in the towers at each corner of the camp could direct fire and light to anywhere in the camp and the twin barbed wire front gates were never opened at the same time. Also what seemed to be a regiment of guards and dogs patrolled regularly inside and outside the wire. On the ground between the fences in the ten foot gap, were three coils of barbed wire, one on top of two others stretched out in concertina fashion, making any escape bid in this direction virtually impossible. A pretty tight camp.

Our reception met with the same old routine, the German camp commandant reading the Dos and Don'ts of the camp, in German, while an interpreter read the same old rubbish in English. It all boiled down to one thing; everything was forbidden. We were fed up with hearing it, we called it the riot act, and as soon as the commandant started everyone yelled out 'We know *alles verboten*!'

The intake was thoroughly organized, as the lorries entered and unloaded, the prisoners were taken to a long brick built building, strip searched, asked a few questions, then ordered to fall in outside, prior to being allocated huts. I was told of an amusing incident that occurred during our strip search. One of the prisoners had a long minor bullet would in his buttock, covered with a thick wad of cotton wool plastered over it. He told his searchers, through an interpreter, that the dressing must not be removed for another two days: doctor's orders. He was passed through into the redressing room, whereupon, four of his mates seized him, ripped off the plaster and retrieved sundry pound and ten shilling notes. They had lain hidden amid the cotton wool all the way from the last camp.

Within an hour of being searched, we had all been allocated huts. By now we were all experienced at resettling in new camps and it didn't take long to become acquainted with the guards, who in the main, were a pretty friendly lot and not adverse to a little bit of barter trading. This mainly took place at night between ourselves and the internal guards, who were in collusion with the guards patrolling the outer fence. Their routine became so familiar we could almost tell where they would be at any given time, we also had to cater for the guard dogs. To pacify the dogs, small morsels of corned beef or other meat foods from our parcel were taken down to the wire. These titbits were collected from each prisoner wishing to barter that night, and on arrival at the inner fence were presented to the dogs who eventually became less vicious which allowed us to approach the guard freely.

Our system of barter was simple, and in use throughout the camp. Any unwanted item from our food parcel we could not swap among ourselves or could forgo was itemized and a list passed clandestinely to the guard. Usually the first evening guard to come on duty would leave a list of the articles they hoped to obtain, and their barter value. A rota was drawn up so every hut had a first chance down at the wire, this enabled everyone the priority and option of what was going. Four representatives from each hut collected their hut's wares, then assembled in our hut after evening roll call, this hut being the nearest to the wire. The main article in demand by us was bread, and by the Germans, cigarettes, chocolate, and LUX toilet soap, although all manner of items changed hands. The soap and chocolate were in most cases, kept to give to their girlfriends and wives. Canadian coffee was very highly priced on the barter market, but many Germans would not, or could not, pay the asking price. As usual there were some who at times jeopardized the system by cheating on a barter and, invariably, it was one of our men.

Our con-artists were adept in doctoring articles to be traded. Cocoa for instance, cinders from the compound were ground into powder, then mixed thoroughly with approximately half a tin of cocoa powder. To determine the correct weight, an unopened tin was used as a balance, the tin's bottom, which had been carefully removed was then resealed, and the tin passed off as genuine. Doctoring the soap was a work of art. All it needed was a razor blade, a steady hand, and a little patience. The bar to be operated on was cut round the sides and parted, the inside of each half was carefully cut out, the cavities refilled with German ersatz soap. To reseal the bar, both halves were moistened and pressed tightly together, and allowed to dry, then re-packed so expertly it looked as though it had just arrived from the manufacturers. The tea for barter was genuine, only it had been brewed a number of times and dried out, then replaced into the packet with a technician's touch. In fact, every conceivable fiddle the prisoners could work, and get away with, they did.

One such artist eventually engineered his own downfall, he was caught taking a packet of genuine unopened tea from another prisoner's food parcel, and replacing it with doctored tea. An inquiry presided over by the camp leader decided it was stealing, the punishment was pretty dire. I had seen punishment dealt out before, by camp court martial, but this was diabolical. The offender was thrown into one of the camp's cesspools, and with two brooms, ducked twice, on the second ducking he was held under for a longer period. He was then dragged out with the help of the brooms, and left to cleanse himself the best way he could. On his return to the hut he still reeked of excreta, and was made to sleep outside that night surely saving him from further punishment. This insane form of punishment was then banned by the camp commandant, as quite rightly, it constituted a health threat to the whole camp.

11

As in all camps, everyone sooner or later pals up with another person to become muckers, that is except the out-and-out loners. This often led to an exchange of bunks, when possible, although the term 'bunk' was an over statement. In our hut they were just two tier shelves, protruding some five and a half feet on two sides, built integral with the hut walls. There was a trestle table, a wood burning stove, which, to my knowledge, was never alight. There were no mattresses, and only one blanket issued per man.

During one such switch around I palled up with a fellow about my own age. We managed to procure part of the bottom shelf, apart from it being less trouble to keep tidy, it was a lot warmer. One night well after lights out, a small new intake arrived, which was unusual, normally any prisoners arriving after dark would stay the night in the detention block, for security reasons. Two of the new chaps had been allocated to our hut, and left in the darkness to fend for themselves. They groped around for a place to kip down for the night and my mate, without asking me, offered to share our part of the shelf with one of them, who gladly accepted. I wondered how the hell the three of us could kip in such cramped conditions.

That problem solved itself, we had just settled down for the night, when this new chap started to feel amorous, and put his hand on my chest, although I was fully clothed my tunic was open, he fumbled with my shirt trying to feel my nipple. I soon put that sex starved bastard in his place. I confronted him in a threatening manner, timidly he apologized, saying it was an accident. Accident was right, he had picked on the wrong person, I had a job to restrain myself from walloping him there and then. So to avoid a punch-up, which would bring in the guards, I moved to the upper shelf. Next morning I found I was on my own once more, my mate had deserted me in favour of the new arrival, who was giving orders, well he thought he was, as to how our food parcels should be shared out. As yet, he had not been issued with one. Later that morning they both moved to another part of the hut, not just as buddies, but lovers. I was glad to be rid of them.

The camp concert party put an excellent variety show on for us one night, the auditorium was full to capacity, also enjoying the gaiety that night, was the camp commandant, and many of the off duty guards. Everybody enjoyed the night's entertainment, at the conclusion of which, all the performers received a standing ovation. Some of the performers had dressed up as women, as one or two of the acts called for female characters. Between acts, one of the female impersonators was forced to use the toilets at the far end of the camp and was halted by a guard who mistook him for a woman visitor. While being escorted to the gates, was told, only young ladies with escorts are admitted to the camp concerts. Unfortunate for him, if he had not been questioned at the gate by another guard, who asked for the Fraulein's papers, he would have walked away to freedom.

Another incident occurred while I was an unwilling guest in Stalag IIa. I was badgered, cajoled, and finally goaded into taking part in a football match between two huts. The unbeatable hut 16 challenged our hut, (R.A.F. and weather permitting). I had never followed the game, my knowledge of it restricted to memories of rough schoolboy kick-abouts in the playground, and feared the worst.

The weather turned fairly warm, (it would). I had hoped it would pour with rain, so the game would be cancelled. As usual the worst happened. Towards the final minutes of the goalless match, I was bunched up in the opposing goal mouth, awaiting a corner kick. As I was the smallest player on the field, my view of play was limited and most of the other players towered above me. A whistle sounded but no one moved, after a minute or so I jumped up to try and see what was happening. The ball came at me like a bloody bullet, I shut my eyes and turned my head very quickly, as to avoid a direct hit to my face, I was knocked out for a while. When I came round the match was over, and I was being feted like a hero. Apparently, after knocking me out, the ball went ricocheting into the goal giving our side the victory. I made sure I was not around to be picked on again for any other blinking football matches in future.

Six of us were detailed for tin bashing, i.e. tins from the food parcels had to be compressed for easy disposal, after flattening a few tins we were told to report to the theatre hut, most of the camp had assembled there. A German officer was making an appeal to the camp in general for volunteers to work on what he said would be a new annex to the camp, affording better facilities for all prisoners. The foundations of this building had already been laid, and with our help it was hoped construction would be speeded up. We would be paid twenty pfennigs per day, (Lager Geld) which was useless for any purchases I had in mind, in fact, useless for anything else, even bum paper. Our suspicions about this new annex were later confirmed, we were being conned.

In fact the new building was for a factory, but many of us, including myself, volunteered, to make a break from prison routine, also, perhaps, prison life. With better weather approaching this would be an ideal job for the long summer months, without necessarily speeding up construction.

The idea was short lived. After ten days we were back in camp confined to routine chores like tin bashing and window cleaning. The prisoners who the camp commandant picked as the ring leaders, although he never had proof, had to fill in the camp's latrines and dig new ones. In those ten days as bricklayers and labourers, the acts of sabotage had become so blatant they could no longer pass as accidents, and it was a wonder no one was shot for their actions.

An uproar started when a group of prisoners were given tins of red paint, and ordered to stencil KG (Kriegsgefangner) and a three inch triangle on all the backs of the British P.O.W.s' battle dresses. Amidst this wild fracas, most of the tins of paint was lost by being turned upside down onto the

50

ground, or kicked over deliberately. After the heated hassle had been quelled, the camp commandant receded, and detailed his off duty guards the unwanted chore.

It was at this time, a simple but ingenious idea was circulating through the camp. It was for a small heating stove that was nothing more than a hand operated forge. Although the weather was now quite warm, our experiences during the previous winter months had led one bright spark to dream up this innovation (known to kriegies as the blower). The inadequate heating in the huts restricted us cooking or warming food and in the winter our food was almost stone cold by the time we had got it back to the hut. Permission had been granted for us to build small fires during the day in approved spots but there was always a shortage of kindling and burning materials. This stove or forge consisted of a short wooden base, approximately eighteen inches by seven inches, part of a bunk board when obtainable was ideal. Two Klim tins were joined together, without lids with the top tin's bottom well perforated and the bottom tin slotted out on one side, to house a cocoa tin. This made the fire box. Another smaller round tin housed a four bladed fan, making the wind chamber, the fire box and the wind chamber was then connected by a bottomless and topless cocoa tin. A short upright at one end to support a drive wheel, by which means of a drive belt, string or boot lace, the fan turned. When turned the fan would create a draft into the fire box. The fire box would be lined with clay, when available. Once the fire box was alight, cooking was no problem, tea or coffee took only a few minutes to make. Old cardboard food boxes, empty cigarette packets, wood, when obtainable, even cinders from the compound, all made excellent burning material. The only snag was we were not allowed to operate these Blowers inside the hut, or outside after dark. If found doing so, the whole lot, blower, and food would be smashed, by the guard's boots or rifle butt.

I cannot recall if it was in this camp, Stalag IIa, or in a previous one, that I first encountered Russian prisoners. I remember a little compound containing three largish huts, which almost covered the whole area, I did not see the full complement of Russian prisoners, but there were a few hundred of them. Those who were seen in the small compound, were unkempt, starving, wretches, their faces drawn looking like a bag of bones. The Geneva Convention did not apply to them, therefore no Red Cross parcels were ever issued to them. Mostly the Germans treated them like dirt, giving them the leftovers and scraps, not consumed by other prisoners. We did our best to throw portions of our food over the tall partitioning barbed-wire fence to them when we could, if seen doing so by the guard, we were liable to be shot.

We never saw any guard dogs put into the Russian compound, rumour had it that one dog had already vanished, only its fleshless bones were found buried in the compound. The guards would not venture near the fearsome huts alone.

Suddenly security became far more strict, the guards more aloof, and we were subjected to annoying unexpected strip searches by arrogant guards, and on two occasions I can recall, a civilian was present, most probably the Gestapo. Blackout precautions were tightened up, although as yet, there had been no Allied air raids over this area of Germany. I had been in this camp now almost eight weeks, and had seen two or three of my mates leave for working parties. I thought I was a permanent resident, until I was told to report for another search along with a group of other prisoners, we expected another random search, but after a quick once-over, we were loaded on to lorries, with the usual armed guard. Our destination being, we were told, various working camps. As we moved out we noticed all the guards had been doubled, and a light armoured car outside, facing the camp gates, we knew something was going on. We stopped a way down the road to allow a long mechanized convoy of troops to pass, we then overtook companies of infantry men all full battle order, all heading in the same direction. We wondered what the hell was happening. We found out on arrival at our new camp, that morning we had left Stalag IIa had been 6 June, 'D' Day, the Allied invasion of France.

12

Arbeits Kommando 544/9 was a working camp, comprising of one long brick-built building, a solitary confinement cell, and surface air-raid shelter. It was situated on the outskirts of Magdeburg, Germany. The building was divided into ten medium-size rooms, six of which contained five two-tiered bunks, that still left ample room to move about. Also, at the far end of the building was a stores room, and another room which was the officers' quarters. Six of the first rooms housed the prisoners, the next room on the left was the guards' quarters, which seemed to be larger than the other rooms. How this room was furnished I had no idea. Directly opposite the guards' quarters, was the prisoners' ablutions, the windows here, and in the prisoners' rooms, were unglazed, with thick iron bars set parallel in the brickwork, all of which had wooden shutters fitted to the outside. The shutters served as blackout panels at night, which were opened and shut by the guard on duty.

The rooms were clean, apart from the wood shavings which still littered the concrete floor. The whole structure of this ground floor building appeared to have been recently built, we were the first occupants. The camp was surrounded by just one high barbed-wire fence, and with only a few guards in residence, there were no guard dogs, and no lookout towers, and was patrolled night and day by only two guards, one on either side of the wire. The camp was run by a middle-aged German officer, whose knowledge of English was excellent, and could converse with the best of us, although he very rarely did so. On one side of the camp were disused and over-grown allotments, our back view overlooked open grassland. A narrow well-trodden footpath ran about ten feet parallel to the back barbed wire fence, once most probably a short cut to the now overrun allotments, but now used by the civilians as an advantage point, to gloat at us Englander schwein hund. From the camp's small barbed wire front gate, a cart track gave access to the main road, beyond which, open fields stretched down to the river Elbe. On our fourth side, about seventy yards away, was a large tall almost isolated building which proved to be a furniture factory, owned by a Herr Stossmeister. Other smaller buildings stood some hundred and fifty yards away, and seemed uninhabited.

Out of our group, which totalled sixty, all from Stalag IIa, the majority were allocated to the furniture factory which was producing utility chairs, tables, desks, beds, and bunks. The day after our arrival we were duly escorted by our guard to Herr Stossmeister's empire, where an oldish grey-haired German foreman, named Andy (of all names) tried painfully to explain our duties. There was to be no payment for our work, and we would work the same hours as the German civilian staff. Resume work promptly after meal breaks which will also be the same as the staff, but we soon found out, same meal breaks but not the same meals. Our nourishment came in the form of ersatz coffee, we had to wait till our watery soup and meagre bread ration were given out at nighttime in camp.

Always in the factory we had three armed guards in attendance, while a fourth guard roamed the factory grounds. I'm afraid very little was achieved by us for the German war effort that first day, or any other day come to that, I'm glad to say. As we discussed the day's events on return to camp we found various contacts had been made with the German staff, in view to establishing a barter agreement, namely, English fags for German bread. Our own bread ration in camp had been reduced to one small standard size loaf per eight men a day, which at first each room member had to take his turn, to cut and issue out. Thankfully this unpopular chore was taken over by the room leader. To ensure a reasonable supply of barter bread, our cigarette resources had to suffer, and eventually dwindle so low, it meant forgoing the pleasure of a cigarette. Each of the little rooms had its own small wood burning stove, which allowed us to heat up an impromptu meal or drink, when and if possible. At lights-out each night our trousers and boots were confiscated, and locked in a large cupboard in the store room, at the end of the building, then returned to us in the morning, or if the air raid warning sounded. This chore was executed by two men from each room, who took these articles down and returned to their respective rooms, carrying the inevitable emergency toilet container. The same pair would reverse the procedure in the morning, returning the toilet container first, which from our room, to my knowledge was never used. Obviously, this nightly routine although very annoying, was all done to discourage any escape bid.

Our work at the factory varied as we were switched from one task to another, but the bulk of production centred mainly around the wood lamination press. This produced the large sheets of blockboard, from which many of the furniture items were made, especially table and desk tops. The making of these blockboards consisted of slats of soft wood of various lengths, up to some seven feet long. The three-quarter inch square wood slats were laid on a thin sheet of rough pre-glued wood, approximately six foot by four foot, and butted against each other, the shorter lengths were also butted end to end, then tightly packed together in a large vice jig. To complete the operation, the slats were smeared with glue and an identical thin sheet of wood was placed on top. When six such sheets had been assembled, they were stacked on top of each other in the press, and with the press ram closed down on them overnight, they were ready for use next morning, after being cut to the required size.

My introduction to this task fell deliberately short of the day's target, and back in camp I was threatened with a week's solitary confinement. This punishment was then altered, for two nights, after work, for about an hour or so, I was made to break up red house bricks into small chippings, with which some inane German wanted to create his army divisional emblem on top of our air raid shelter. Set in a cinder background, with the prominent feature made with small round cheese tins from our English Red Cross food parcels, it was highlighted by the red brick. The magnitude of such a sign would be visible to aircraft miles away, apparently an open invitation to the Allied planes to bomb it.

Andy, the German foreman was a decent old fellow who tried to help us the best he could, knowing full well we had no intentions of taking work seriously. His usual sign of disapproval was to point his index finger upwards in a circular movement, at the same time shaking his thinning grey head from side to side. He was becoming aware, as were we all, that the war was going against the Germans, and had resigned himself to the inevitable. There was one job at the factory we all set about with gusto. An order had come through for an unlimited amount of three tier bunks, which, it was rumoured, were destined for the German Luftwaffe. This was given priority, and all our group were assigned to the project. The bunks had two stout longitudinal wood members that supported the wooden slats, and took the entire weight of the user. Specification insisted these members be glued and strongly nailed in position, and in the case of the bottom bunk they were. On the upper bunks though we cut off the nail heads, which when driven home just through the supports and obviously had no holding power. We used no glue except a smear over the outer joints to fool the inspectors who arrived regularly to check our progress. All that held the longitudinal members were four well positioned nails.

Inspection of the bunks included treading hard on the bottom bunk, but giving the top two bunks a sharp blow with their fists, which we had already proved they could withstand. They were then satisfied, and so were we, knowing that with the full weight of a man on them they would collapse, with probably dire results to the bottom occupant. We could imagine the chaos these bunks would cause amongst the returning German aircrews, especially those just returned from a long bombing mission. We refrained writing on the bunks, 'Made in Germany by British prisoners of war' as we did on some of the tables and desks which left Herr Stossmeister's factory.

Our camp leader had found out there was a de-lousing unit

some half a mile from camp, and although we were now clear of vermin, (lice) he decided it would do us no harm to be treated. This would also get us out of camp, also away from work for a few hours. He therefore made arrangements with the camp commandant for us to attend, and next morning first thing after roll call, we were mustered outside the camp, and with almost all the guards we marched to the unit. While we showered our clothes were fumigated, on leaving the showers we were told to raise our arms sideways to shoulder height, and walk with our legs wide apart, spread-eagle fashion, and walk in a single file. We were made to pass an elderly woman (her appearance resembled that of a Russian woman), whose thin frail frame was enveloped in what seemed like a tattered army blanket. She had before her a large tub of brownish fluid, which looked like creosote, and she held what looked like a toilet brush in her wrinkled, shaking hand. As each man passed he received three deft dabs with the brush, one under each arm and once under the crutch and genitals. She operated as though she had done it all her life. The fluid burnt like hell, and getting dressed only aggravated the situation, but marching back to camp, for the first two hundred yards was sheer torture. We wondered which had been the worse, the lice, or the de-lousing. If there had been any vermin that had escaped the hot showers, they would certainly have been burnt to death by this stuff. Had we known the outcome of this farce, I doubt if anyone would have bothered.

13

Although I had written home at regular intervals during my seven months of captivity I had never received any reply. Then one morning the camp leader shouted 'Mail up lads, come and get it!' There was just one mad eager rush. On hearing my name called I yelled 'Over here!' and was handed a letter. I opened it with some trepidation, expecting the worst. My fears were unjustified, all at home were okay and the delay was explained. My mother was only now receiving letters written by me months ago, when at that time she was officially notified I was missing, presumed dead, and was now overjoyed to hear from me. Her letter boosted my morale no end, and the monotonous isolation of prison life seemed easier to bear. As her letter was rigidly censored, I could get no idea of how conditions were back home, but I contented myself with the assumption that they could be no worse right now than conditions in Germany. As soon as I had finished my evening meal, I wrote a letter in reply letting them know I had received theirs okay and I was alright, and in good health, not for them to worry about me, as I could cope with the situation.

It was an open secret now that Germany was being held on the Russian front and retreating slowly on the Western front, and all manner of rumours were circulating throughout both the camp and factory. One such rumour suggested that the Gestapo was searching all P.O.W. camps for British army pay books, to be used by undercover squads masquerading as British soldiers and infiltrating the allied front in France. To hide our own, one of our men, a skilled cabinet maker, with the help of some more prisoners, made for them who wanted them, small shaving kit boxes with sliding lids. The bottom was made from two thin pieces of oak veneer glue-sealed together, between which was also sealed our army pay books.

This was my task. To identify each individual box, a prisoner with an artistic flair, would for a cigarette, colour a Walt Disney character, or any other symbol on the lid, whatever the owner wanted. The finished box, when varnished, made a very handy and attractive looking box. The boxes were left lying around in our rooms, on a small shelf at the foot of our bunks, without any attempt of concealment. Later on we were in fact searched by two guards, accompanied by the camp commandant, and two miserable looking civilians. It was a pretty routine affair, so straightforward, I doubt if I have ever witnessed an easier search, and no demand was made of us to produce our army pay books.

A few days after the search, we had a visit from the German branch of the Red Cross Organization; who chatted to us in a friendly and open manner. They enquired as to our treatment as P.O.W.s, also were we receiving the Red Cross food parcels regularly. We told them our treatment was tolerable, which was true, and the food parcels were a godsend, as from the first week at this working camp, every man had received one food parcel each week. As the conversation progressed, they asked about our leisure hours, we replied there is not much we can do, only wait and hope. They promised to send us a table tennis outfit and a dart board, also packs of playing cards, which to everyone's surprise, they did. The snag was there was no room for the table tennis outfit, inside or outside. When the weather was at all reasonable the small compound would be crowded. Nevertheless we had the dart board to while away the time, till the German guards confiscated the two sets of darts as possible weapons for use against them. So eventually we finished up with an unused dart board, and packets of playing cards.

Another working party of ten men, left the camp half an hour before us each morning, they worked, (well played at it) for a Herr Jacob. The main product was reinforced concrete slabs for road blocks. The lengths of iron rods which would be used in the reinforcement were substituted. The guards were shown the iron rods placed on the surface of the wet cement base, two or three of the lads would create a diversion

59

this enabled the rods to be removed, and to interpolate straw, or twigs from the nearby bushes. A thin layer of concrete was then spread over the top, forming a fine corrugated pattern, the guards were then invited to inspect it again, which they mostly ignored, or after a quick look just walked away. One of the prisoners jumped on to a finished slab, and it just disintegrated, the pieces were craftily concealed amongst other rubble, awaiting disposal. How they managed to turn out such inferior masterpieces undetected, without reprisals being taken, remained a mystery. None of the slabs made by our British prisoners were ever used while we stayed at Magdeburg. The only persons to benefit from this escapade were the prisoners, who could get out of the camp daily, and barter for bread, or other food stuffs.

A change of routine occurred when I was one of a party of four picked for a trip to Magdeburg railway sidings, our task was to unload a consignment of wood urgently needed by Herr Stossmeister. Two of us unloaded from the long open truck, while another two reloaded the wood on an open back lorry, while our guard sat inside the cab talking to the driver. Chances of getting into town were nil, and as daylight air raids were becoming more imminent, we decided to put our backs into the task and get out of the marshalling yard as fast as possible.

We finished the job by early afternoon, and as the lorry drove away we commenced our march back to the factory. Approaching a small beer garden, our guard stopped us and made a gesture as if holding a glass to his mouth indicating we were invited to a drink, to which we all agreed. He led us into a small room at the rear of the beer garden and ordered five glasses of lager, then left us to resume his conversation with the landlord, taking his glass with him. The ice-cold beer was appreciated, and it tasted very good, probably because we hadn't tasted any since leaving England, and we took our time drinking it, our guard returned and joined us at the table. One of our team had picked up a smattering of German, through him, our guard told us he had served in North Africa, also he had a brother who was now a prisoner of war in Scotland, and he understood how we must feel. We finished our drinks and strolled rather than marched back to the factory, reaching it as the last of the timber was being unloaded from the lorry, the oak veneer being very carefully stored in the factory basement.

That night we heard a few explosions, but no one had any idea what they were, some sounded very close, and shook the camp violently, shaking us in our bunks. Rumours started as to what the explosions were, the first being, the Germans were blowing the bridges across the river Elbe, another, troops had been dropped, and were blowing up vital installations, the third, which was true, a few bombs had been dropped.

The following morning, two other prisoners and myself with one guard, were taken off our factory duties, to clear rubble from a building some hundred and fifty yards from the factory. When the three of us arrived at the small building we could see it had been almost demolished by a direct hit, during the previous night's air-raid. Two overfed pompous German civilians seemed to be in charge of the operations, seemingly they were eagerly telling our guard what we must do, their main concern to gain access to the basement, which was blocked with a huge pile of rubble. We worked for two days before clearing a path to the steps and a safe entrance down to the basement, and the two civilians, who must have been informed of our progress, immediately descended to investigate. They returned minutes later and spoke excitedly to our guard, while brushing invisible dust from their immaculate tailor-made attire, then drove off in a chauffeur driven car. Apart from a very thick layer of dust, and other varied debris, also a massive gap in the ceiling, which admitted our only light, a major part of the basement was still intact. The place was stacked almost ceiling high with boxes of glass tubes, all shapes, sizes, and graduations, some cracked, others smashed to pieces, and others surprisingly untouched, this was our quarry. We cleared a good space on the basement floor, then put sacking and corrugated cardboard down to protect the valuable unbroken tubes. We sorted out all the intact tubes in their various shapes and sizes, and markings, which took us two more days. The end result was a work of art, with neat stacks of tubes glistening on the clean corrugated cardboard. This salvage job now almost finished, pleased the two arrogant Germans who had paid us an unexpected visit. Our main concern was how to arrange for the 'accidental' demolition of this work of art, as one pile appeared to be of prime importance to the two civilians.

Leaning against the basement wall directly behind our artistic display, was a massive slab of brickwork, which we had previously manhandled in to to this position, for no apparent reason, apart from giving us access to the basement. Behind the base of this slab lay more rubble. We filled a box with mostly broken tubes, placed a few undamaged tubes on top, and replaced a partly torn lid, then removed some of the rubble from behind the slab, placed the box in a shallow hole leaving one torn corner visible, then replaced most of the rubble. Our next move was to call the guard down and show him what we had accomplished, he had been driven outside by the dust, a good excuse for him to have a smoke. He approved of our fine work, and told us, mainly by gestures, that we were now finished here. At this point, one of our team shouted and pointed to the box we had planted, 'Look there is another box full over there!' We all crowded around the brick slab, guard as well. 'Ja, das ist gut,' he mumbled. The three of us then began to inch the slab away from the wall to get to the partly buried box. Our guard seeing us struggling, propped his rifle against a remaining wall, and came to assist, but was not quick enough. One man had already climbed onto the pile of rubble behind the slab, and with his hands against the wall, backed the slab into an upright position, giving the guard the impression one of us would retrieve the box, whereupon the massive lump of brickwork commenced a sickly wobble, and amid murderous cries of, 'Watch it you bloody fool!' and 'We can't hold the bloody thing!' Then the pre-arranged word, 'Right!' We executed our plan, we jumped clear as it crashed down smashing the tubes to smithereens, the sound of shattered glass was like music to our ears. Out of the many hundreds of assorted tubes, we salvaged a little over a hundred from the glass covered floor, all the time berating our third man with our foulest language, for the benefit of the guard. Who being amongst us at the time, and almost flattened, believed our outburst to be genuine. To dispute our claim this disaster was not an accident, and to inform his superiors of such, the chances are, he would be sent to the Russian front, or shot, for negligence of his duties, especially in a case of sabotage. As he had, by his actions to help us, made himself an active member in this affair.

14

The food situation had now reached an all-time low, especially the bread ration, one small army loaf between eight men, and our barter trade was now essential. Our Red Cross food parcels started coming at irregular intervals, sometimes three or four weeks would go by without us receiving any, then it was one parcel between two.¹ The camp commandant was by now well aware that barter trade was taking place between prisoners, guards, and civilians, and were making attempts to stem it. The shortage of food parcels meant no cigarette issue, and all cigarette parcels from home were confiscated, and re-issued at twenty cigarettes per day to the owner, on the assumption that he would be left with insufficient to barter with. The commandant issued orders that no man was allowed to take more than three cigarettes out of the camp each day. As most of our bartering for bread was with civilians at the factory, this was drastic news.

As usual, when cigarettes were available, we overcame this problem. By slitting the button holes of our epaulettes we could tuck three cigarettes in each (one of my ideas) without crushing after re-buttoning. So with our allowance of three cigarettes in the packet, which were shown to the gate guard, sometimes, each man could smuggle out nine fags per day. A civvy loaf normally cost ten full size cigarettes, so between two of us we had ample to bargain with and enough for a smoke. In the main stalag cigarettes before being traded would in some cases, have been docked approximately a quarter of an inch, but here we depended on this bread barter, so doctoring anything by anyone was forbidden. We were allowed to bring sacks of scrap wood from the factory each night to stoke the wood burning stoves, and any bread we had managed to get was hidden between the wood and smuggled through the gate guard. As we approached the gate, we would hold up the sacks saying, '*Holz für der feuer*,' they knew what was in the sacks, but didn't stop us, as many of them were bartering with us themselves.

I was now right out of cigarettes; no more bartering for me for the present. Things were looking rather black for us and, as my mate was in the same boat, we could just hope for the best. Next morning, Friday the Thirteenth, proved a lucky day. I received a cigarette parcel from home, five hundred Player's Weights, my favourite smoke, from an elder brother. Although confiscated on arrival, my twenty cigarettes per day kept me, and my non-smoker mate in bread, and me in smokes for over a month.

A London chappie also received a cigarette parcel that day, and seeing my Player's Weights pleaded with me to swop ten of them for twenty of his Royalty, as Weights were the only fag he really enjoyed. I was in full agreement but offered him a straight swop, ten for ten, as one Royalty was more than equal to two Player's Weights, and the butt would make a reasonable size resmoke. He still insisted on the two for one basis, saying he did not mind being the loser over the deal as it was worth it just this once to get a decent smoke and he had received twice the amount of cigarettes that I had. On our way back to our respective rooms, he thanked me again, saying he was very grateful, yet it was me who really profited from our transaction.

It was now late autumn, and with the prospects of long winter months ahead with reduced rations, increasing air raids, and another Christmas behind barbed wire, everyone, including the Germans, was becoming war weary, and in our case prison weary. I gained some small consolation from the fact that I had only been in captivity just over a year, whereas some of the chaps had spent four years perhaps more behind the wire. Having to look at barbed wire that length of time, day after day, proved beyond endurance for some, they become nervous wrecks. With the run up to Christmas, Allied air activity increased, and we were spending more night hours in the cold damp air raid shelter, with the massive German army divisional sign on top, than in our bunks. What made it

65

worse was having to wait for our trousers and boots to be given to us before dashing to the shelter, sometimes half naked. This was happening almost every night now, most of the chaps said *sod it*, and stayed in the room, against repeated threats from the guard. Having to sort out boots and trousers, nine times out of ten in the dark, was one big balls-up. Mostly, you finished up with someone else's clobber on, or two odd boots, causing a humiliating situation.

At Christmas, 1944, we were given two days off from the factory and with everyone in the camp receiving a Canadian food parcel, we hoped to make it far more pleasant than the last. The guards seemed to relax and become more friendly during this period, and brought us in some German wine diluted with weak lemonade, which we all enjoyed. So we did have a drink of something to celebrate Christmas, if it was non-alcoholic. We also over-indulged ourselves from our food parcels, after dinner I regaled the lads with my bartered mouth organ, though not up to Larry Adler standards. They joined in with the carols and soon all the camp, including the guards, were belting out 'Silent Night' and 'Noel' at the top of their voices. I was requested to play 'Silent Night' again for two of the guards, who stood outside the open shuttered window and sang, they each rewarded me with a cigarette.

The next day, Boxing Day, the German commandant, temporarily imbued with the festive spirit, had classical music, including songs by Tauber, played over the camp's loudspeaker system, although subdued, the haunting melodies released the suffering from our minds and replaced it with thoughts of better days. We were also given New Year's Day off, but after that it was back to the old monotonous camp life, and dreary factory routine.

The New Year gave us all a new hope for peace. We thought this war cannot go on very much longer, someone must throw in the towel soon. I had abandoned all ideas of escaping a long time ago, so had a majority of prisoners in our camp. It would be an insane act to try, no advantage could be gained now, and the possibility of getting maimed or killed was very high. As I talked to many of my fellow prisoners I sensed that what had deterred most of them from escaping, was lack of the German language, inability to stock enough food for the journey, and, as there was no escape committee in this camp, maps, travelling permits and money was impossible to obtain. One old-timer I spoke to said, '*It looks like the war is nearing its end, and after three and a half years behind the wire, I'm bloody certain I can put up with it for another six months or so. It's a foregone conclusion that the Allied troops will be here soon, so I'm quite content to stay here and wait for them.*'

The monotonous days dragged on; week after week of unadulterated boredom. Then on the night of 16 January 1945 we had just got our heads down for the night when our fears materialized. This time when the air raid siren sounded a sense of danger filled the room and there was the usual mad dash for the trousers and boots. As we headed for the shelter I heard the drone of bombers approaching and marker flares beginning to fall. On seeing the flares, the chaps who normally ignored air raid warnings, grabbed at anyone's trousers and boots, regardless of size, making them look ridiculous, with trousers almost up to their knees and boot sizes too big. Someone yelled, 'Come on you lot it looks like we'll get it tonight' and more men ran out with boots and trousers tucked under their arms their bare bottoms dancing and flashing in the darkness. We had barely reached the shelter when the sickening and deafening crunch of bombs seemed to lift the shelter bodily, as we were thrown in a scared, jumbled heap on the floor covered with dust. We sat there, a frightened cowering mass as more near misses rained down outside, shaking the shelter, and showering us with fragments of concrete falling from the roof. Nevertheless, the shelter remained intact, and the sound of exploding bombs became less nerve-shattering as the Allied planes throbbed onward to their main target; Magdeburg.

It must have been almost half an hour before the last wave of bombers passed overhead, and we risked leaving the shelter, only to find that apart from the shelter, the camp no longer existed. The commandant's pet Alsatian had been

67

trapped in the officers' quarters and to save it a painful, agonizing death it was shot by its master. By the grace of God, and to everybody's amazement, there were no casualties throughout the entire camp. What little remained of the main building was blazing merrily, sparks ascending like fireflies in the smoke filled night air. The compound was scattered with miscellaneous articles, a large bomb crater, and long stretches of barbed wire were gone. A mile to the east of us lay Magdeburg, it was a clear night, and we could see a large pall of smoke over the town like a blanket of death, supported by the heat from the raging fires beneath, conjuring up a scene direct from hell. Most of the small buildings around our factory, including Herr Stossmeister's appeared to be well alight, and the smell of burning was everywhere. (A participant on that raid informed me some forty years later that it was a fire raid, consisting of seventy per cent incendiary bombs, the remainder, H.E. and delayed action bombs.)

We were assembled into some kind of order, and a roll call taken, then ordered back down the shelter, which was the only place left to house us. Here we remained through the long dark hours, dwelling on the fact that everything we possessed had gone up in smoke.

15

At first light next morning the whole camp was assembled on what was once the camp compound, now littered with burnt wood, bricks, and a mound of earth. All that existed of the camp was the shell, and a few inner walls, and blackened heaps of smouldering charcoal, lengths of flattened barbed wire lay scattered everywhere. Some of the larger beams of wood were still alight, and other smaller pieces had small flames dancing on top of them, with their fiery tongues licking the sides, trying to consume every inch. Another roll call was taken, after which, the entire camp complement was marched to the furniture factory, which on close inspection, had received no structural damage apart from windows blasted out by the very near misses. Here the smell of damp smouldering wood dominated the area. The large wood store behind the factory and two out buildings however, had received direct hits by incendiary bombs, and were still well alight, with Herr Stossmeister and most of his staff trying to quench the flames. Two of us were ordered to check the top floor of the factory, which was glass-strewn, but otherwise okay. From the glassless windows, the huge black cloud could still be seen hanging over the terror stricken town.

The wood store was a large open structure with a corrugated steel roof. The blast from a near miss H.E. bomb had torn part of the roof away, and had hurled corrugated sheets and planks of wood in all directions. What was left of the wood stores was now being consumed by the incendiary bombs, making it a blazing inferno. We were instructed to help with the fire-fighting, noticing a marked attitude of aloofness by the factory staff towards us. We realized that some of them had homes in Magdeburg, and had possibly suffered great loss from the air raid.

By midday the outside fires were under control, and the

live embers being dampened down. The smoke filled basement appeared to be well alight, our investigations found, it was only smoke which was drifting through the wrecked high basement window, which backed onto the former wood stores. The oak veneer that two of us were told to salvage lay under the window, now just a blackened wooden-surrounded glassless hole. Pieces of window frame and broken glass lay on the top veneer sheet. One fragment of glass had penetrated the veneer to the depth of four sheets, but apart from scorch marks on one sheet, the remaining veneer was undamaged. I should have mentioned that according to Andy, the oak veneer Herr Stossmeister had recently acquired was his quota for six months, and under no circumstances would he receive another consignment. We managed to rake a few live embers through the basement window, and with the draft from the window, and us fanning them we managed to get a sheet of veneer alight. From that we soon had the whole stack of veneer burning furiously. We kept one partly burnt sheet, and, with our eyes streaming, helped by our fingers rubbing them, and a put-on cough, we ascended the stairs to the ground floor. Shaking our heads in mock sympathy we handed Herr Stossmeister the burnt sheet, he was almost in tears himself, but not from smoke. A strong draft caused by the change of wind fed the fire generously, the basement fire was now out of control and burning fiercely. After another three hours of laborious work the fire was extinguished and the basement restored, less the irreplaceable oak veneer.

Apart from ten prisoners and one guard, who were still damping down outside, the entire camp were ordered to go up to the top storey of the factory, to be addressed by the camp commandant.

'After a midday meal, which I have had laid on, you will clean up this room. You will be housed here until further notice.'

With our cabbage-water soup consumed, we set to and made the top floor habitable. Herr Stossmeister came up to supervise in general, and to thank us all for our help in extinguishing the fires. This top room had been used as a lumber store room, and a lot of the junk was unusable. We dropped every piece of this through the bomb blasted windows to the ground to be disposed of by our men below. We then boarded up those windows that were broken, to keep out the rain and frosty winds. Each man marked himself out an ample floor area on which to sleep, for which he was responsible to keep clean and tidy. Herr Stossmeister offered us the use of some of the special three-tiered bunks, from the consignment made for the Luftwaffe.

Although Stossmeister's English was adequate, he spoke in German. The interpreter's translation was, 'Why don't you use the three tiered bunks? There are plenty of them, and they were made by you, so why not use them?' For obvious reasons we gratefully refused, we couldn't say they had been sabotaged, we told him it would be warmer for us sleeping together on the floor.

The room ran the length of the factory and would have housed twice our number. An emergency door leading to a fire escape was one exit from the room, the other accessible door, opened outwards onto a small landing, from which a flight of concrete stairs zigzagged down to the ground floor. Both these doors were locked and bolted every night from the outside, also two armed guards patrolled the factory, one inside around the stairs area, the other one patrolled outside, changing alternately every hour. As we had lost everything except what we wore, we had been re-issued with a blanket, mess tin, and a cheap alloy spoon, these were our total possessions.

It was midwinter and that night was bitterly cold, made worse by the fact that we were in a large upper storey exposed to the elements without any heating. By morning we were cursing that air raid ourselves, the only good thing beneficial to us, which resulted from that raid, was the taking away our boots and trousers which stopped forthwith. If they had been confiscated that night many would have died of exposure.

The following morning while on roll call, we found out we

71

had all been sacked from our factory jobs. Most of the prisoners were assigned to general duties, mostly clearing the factory area in preparation for a new delivery of wood. I believe that a lot of the work was designed to avoid any hostility towards us by Herr Stossmeister's staff over the raid. Our party was detailed as labourers for Magdeburg, clearing rubble.

The route into Magdeburg took us past the large marshalling yards where groups of soldiers and civilians were working amid torn up railway tracks, bomb craters and shattered rolling stock. The cloud of smoke although now not so dense, from remaining fires, still cast a grey shadow over the town. Several little groups of people, mostly old men and women, passed us pushing or pulling hand-carts heaped high with pathetic bundles of salvaged household items. Seeing K.G. stencilled on our backs, some spat at us, the younger ones swore at us and threw pieces of brick or wood picked up from the debris littered road. Although I consoled myself with the fact they were now experiencing what the folk back home had encountered for three years, I felt a strange sense of pity for them, possibly because their plight was much similar to my own.

Deeper into the town we were deployed in separate gangs to clear a path through the completely blocked road. The rubble we shovelled into a horseless cart, which when full, was removed by a group of old men and women, and young girls, some pushing from behind, the remainder pulling on each shaft. There were no horses anywhere in sight, perhaps they had been taken for food which was very scarce. As the cart eventually moved off, a smaller cart looking like an oversize wheelbarrow waited to be loaded. Between the shafts, with a harness over its shoulders was a big Alsatian dog already panting heavily with saliva hanging from its mouth. The destruction to the town as far as we could see, in this area was almost total, and it was rumoured that up to twenty thousand had been killed or injured, and almost the same amount made homeless. Whether this was true or false, we knew that hundreds of aircraft had taken part in the raid, by

72

the successive waves that passed over our shelter that night. We spent the entire day humping and shovelling rubble, and receiving more abuse from the populace. The wealthier a person seemed to be, the most aggressive they were. Perhaps they had suffered a greater financial loss. Our chances to scavenge around for anything edible to augment our now non-existent food reserve back at the factory was nil.

The next day we were split up into smaller groups. The larger group of about fifteen men worked on the road clearance project, two other small groups moved further into the town, while our little group of five were taken to another area, which had once consisted of shops according to the facia signs scattered among the rubble.

We worked with some enthusiasm in hope of unearthing something edible. Unfortunately, all we acquired were aching limbs and a greater hunger. Our guard was a somewhat timid and friendly old boy, who in peacetime would have long-since been pensioned off. He seemed more scared of us than we were of him, allowing us small liberties other guards would have forbidden. The chaps covered for me while I slipped away on the scrounge and after unsuccessful attempts to gain access into a few likely cellars I almost fell down one. Once the thin layer of rubble my foot had gone through, had been removed, a dim light revealed an entrance leading down to a storeroom. Sacks of potatoes and carrots littered the floor. Many looked inedible but about a dozen sacks of each still remained okay and from these I loaded myself up and returned to my workmates. The sliced vegetables were soon cooked to our satisfaction on the long handle shovels held over a blazing fire. The operation was repeated many times until our hunger faded.

The small sack of carrots we smuggled into the factory were shared with our mates, these would be our uncooked breakfast, and give us a little nourishment to help face another day. With the evening's liquid meal (soup) and bread ration consumed, and with nothing to do, we all turned in early, knowing it would take a few hours for us to get warm enough to sleep. The very cold night had been raid-free, which made a pleasant change, our group were up early and very eager to get down to our food supply on the bomb site.

16

Within an hour of arrival at the site, while the others got a fire going, I nipped back to the cellar, returning empty handed and hopelessly discouraged. A bulldozer had cleared that area, blocking the cellar entrance, once more the food situation was back to normal, so was our morale; very low.

It was almost midday and more talk about food had been done than work. Then, as usual, muggins, myself, was selected to reconnoitre for food while the other four kept the old guard occupied. In the side of one pile of masonry I found an opening that appeared to lead to what was once the entrance to a shop. The opening was hidden from the guard's view, so I decided to investigate, although it meant squeezing through a length of unsafe rubble that could easily collapse on me, and the chance of reaching a dead end for my trouble. I inched my way into the darkness for a yard or two, when my leading foot contacted nothing but air, and gingerly groping with the same foot found I was standing at the top of a flight of stairs. I stood hesitating for a minute with one foot on the top step, debating whether to proceed or not, as a cave in would mean almost certain death, either quickly or painfully. I decided to try another step, then another, and I found I could stretch out my arms in all directions without touching anything. I sat down on the third step and continued on my backside, which was a sensible move, as the steps were strewn with small rubble which I cleared away with my feet as I descended. I negotiated ten more steps and found myself sitting on a concrete floor, littered with fallen brickwork, I sat there trying to adjust my eyes to the dusty, gloomy surroundings. The faint glimmer of light from the tunnel entrance only partially penetrated the basement so on hands and knees I groped around to get my bearings. Sweeping a path with a short wide piece of wood as I fumbled about I suddenly bumped my head on what felt like a small stack of cardboard cartons. Further groping revealed they contained tins, the contents of which slopped about when shaken, and as both ends were sealed, they were certainly not paint. The previous day I had found a small sack, which should have been put on the fire, when folded, this fitted into my battle dress pocket unnoticed. I filled the sack with a dozen tins and groped my way to the entrance, only to find the sack was fatter than me, leaving two tins on the stairs, I sidled out through the narrow tunnel.

As none of the tins was marked, I had not the foggiest idea what was in them. Once outside I opened one of the tins, it contained chicken. I started shaking two or three more tins, which all sounded almost the same, I opened another, which contained new potatoes, although fairly small, they had been cooked prior to being canned, as I found out from my first bite. I made my way back to the rest of the chaps, munching a succulent mouthful of cold chicken. I tossed the sack behind a nearby heap of rubble, picked up my shovel and mingled with the group.

My absence had not been noticed by the guard, who was answering the call of nature. This gave me time to tell the chaps of my find, and retrieve the tins. We conned the guard on his return into letting us have a meal break, which two of the chaps had already started. All the tins had been opened, and cooking was in progress over the red hot embers dragged from the enormous fire. Our mess tins had been placed ready to receive the mouth watering feast. What a menu! Chicken, new potatoes, carrots, and a spoonful of garden peas, followed by a plum each.

After a two-hour meal break, work resumed but it was all sham just to keep the guard happy. We decided to take as many of the tins back to the factory as possible, so one of the chaps and myself paid a return visit to the cellar. He didn't like the dicky entrance I had squeezed through, so I left him outside telling him to wait, and I took the small sack from my pocket. Once inside, I filled the sack with tins picked from different areas of the floor, hoping to get a variety of goodies.

76

I made my way back to the entrance, handed the sack through to the chap outside and waited for him to empty it, then I returned and repeated the same operation. We had twenty tins none of which had markings on, so it was impossible to tell what each tin contained. (A few days later I found out some cartons had been labelled stating their contents.)

Getting the tins back to the factory stumped us for a time, but where there's a will, there's a way. We found with our tunic cuff buttoned up, four tins when manipulated into a stacked position, would slip inside the sleeve, the first tin and cuff going into our trouser pocket. With our arm stiffly by our side, inside our trousers we could hold the first tin, then our tunics were buttoned up. This guise gave the impression of having one's hand in one's pocket, the two of us with overcoats had to incorporate the overcoat sleeve in to the plan. To break the uniformity, three had dummy right arms, two had left and as long as we held that first tin in our pocket, and provided we were not thoroughly searched, we could smuggle the twenty tins undetected into the factory. Our luck held, the gate guard just nodded his head as we passed, *eins, zwei, drei, vier, fünf.*

With our move to the factory we maintained our original group of ten. We informed the other five as we spoke in whispers of our El Dorado, and with adroit juggling, smuggled them their share of the loot. In such an open room however, it was impossible to keep a secret, and before morning other prisoners approached us wanting to know the source of our sudden temporary food glut, or more accurately, its location in Magdeburg. Eventually the camp leader conferred with us, and it was agreed that if and when the tins were removed, the proceeds would be shared equally among all sixty P.O.W.s. A small group of prisoners seemed aloof, making them unpopular with the other inmates. The tin food incident brought their self appointed spokesman to the fore, a ginger-haired Scot who could speak fluent French. He spoke with an aggressive assertiveness that jarred the ears, and made me wonder if he was fighting on the wrong side. He would have certainly gone far in the German S.S. He claimed that given the location his team could get the whole lot of the tins back to the factory in one attempt. How he would achieve this he was not asked, nor offered to explain. The camp leader agreed he should try, I did however, explain the dangerous entry, and promised to leave a partly burnt wooden beam, as a marker across the entrance. Then with the aid of the other four in our party, we constructed a rough map of the area for him, and again I emphasized the danger of the unsafe entry.

Next day, back at the rubble heaps we decided to do a repeat of the previous day, and just before midday I cleared off and slid through into the cellar. I selected two tins from the cartons, which according to yesterday's tins from the same cartons, should contain potatoes, plums, and chicken, then I took four more tins from the floor, hoping to get a good variety, my small sack was almost full. I inched my way out, but decided to return by a different route. I wanted to find out what the building next to C&A's had been, in the rubble a dented sign in German caught my eye. I cleared the broken bricks with my foot. Translated, the sign read; 'North Sea Fisheries'. I thought, *tomorrow I'll do a recce in this area, to see what I can find.*

Before getting back to C&A's, our new work site, I encountered large pieces of brickwork and twisted iron girders, making me go on all fours now and then, at times two tins would fall from the sack, I therefore put one in my pocket and awkwardly carried the other. I had just negotiated what seemed like an obstacle course, clambered over a wall, and there I was, face to face with the old guard. He stood there with his rifle pointing at me, and visibly shaking like a leaf, my team mates standing sheepishly behind him. He saw the tin of food in my hand, 'Verboten!' he said, then in broken English, 'I shoot' and he looked so scared he might, if only by accident. I was dead scared also, but forced a grin and said (not knowing if the old fool would understand), 'Oh! would you like a tin, eh?' and tossed the tin in my hand towards him. He automatically dropped his rifle to catch it, and I moved forward and picked it up and, to his amazement, handed it back to him with a grin and patted him on the back. My mates seeing the funny side of it, crowded around him and also patted his back, leaving him utterly bemused and embarrassed. He had taken two bullets from his pocket, and was trying to load his rifle, he looked flummoxed, his fingers were all thumbs, one of the lads calmly took the rifle from our nervous guard, put the two rounds in, and handed the rifle back to him, then jokingly said, '*So he doesn't go and shoot himself, I have put the safety catch on.*' The old boy stood watching us grinning, and eventually assumed we were treating it as a huge joke, and started grinning himself. If this had been a younger more alert guard, we would have been more submissive and cautious, or shot.

We always quit work in Magdeburg about 4.30pm to get us back to the factory before evening roll call. That night, as we approached the factory, the Scotsman and three of his mates had passed through the gates and were going in the direction of Magdeburg. Jock, speaking French, had apparently tricked the guard, who took them for genuine French workmen employees at the factory and let them through. Two of the group were pushing Herr Stossmeister's large wooden hand cart, and all were dressed in borrowed, or stolen French uniforms. Upstairs we asked around, and were told they had gone to get the tins of food, from the cellar on the site, so the rest of us covered for them on roll call. This fact was known only amongst us British prisoners. Should any inquisitive person make inquiries about the French workmen, all one would say was that it's rumoured that they had been detailed to pick up a special consignment of wood for Herr Stossmeister which was urgently needed the next day.

Almost two hours later they returned with the cart piled high with wood. The gate guard, although having been changed, seemed to have been expecting them, as he let them through without hesitation. The cart was pushed to the rear of the factory and unloaded. They had the tins upstairs within minutes, for on our return from an unscheduled roll call, there was not a tin in sight. These were obviously the tins

79

from the cellar in Magdeburg, and the Scotsman had made good his boast. All the British prisoners by this time had been secretly informed regarding the tins of food, and after a few suggestions as to a fair distribution of the loot, it was decided to have a slap up cooked meal on the following Sunday.

In Magdeburg, until now, we had just shovels and a shaky old wheelbarrow to move the rubble, but now mechanical bulldozers were being used in the more congested areas of the town. On our arrival next day we found one operating in our area, and better still, the old guard and the driver knew each other. Owing to yesterday's embarrassing incident the guard had apparently decided to make life easier for himself. He ignored whatever we got up to within reason, at least on the site, knowing full well we would not attempt to escape. This was true, it would be senseless, as the increasing air raids had turned the populace so hostile towards us, we were safer as P.O.W.s, with a guard to protect us. It seemed more sensible to sit it out until the war finished. The old guard and the bull-dozer driver frequently indulged in a debate, and during one of their sessions I slipped away to the cellar to confirm if the tins had gone. They had, I fumbled about in the semi-darkness without finding one tin, making me think; 'Food situation back to normal.' With a disconsolate look I informed the rest of the chaps, who like me, just wished for Sunday to come.

17

That evening, having been locked in for the night, we approached the Scotsman to confirm that he was aware of the decision made about the tins. A murderous air filled the room, when to our amazement he refused to abide by a promise, telling us in his usual aggressive manner, that as four of them had taken all the risk, they were also taking all the spoils. The rest of the room was dumbfounded, and many surged forward with the intent to beat the four up. But the camp leader restrained them. Not one tin was visible in the room and when we asked him where they were hidden, he replied, 'Where you'll not bloody well find them.' The rest of the evening was highly charged, with the foulest of insults being hurled at the Scot and his three mates in the hope of luring them into a fight. But they would not take the bait. This provocation ended eventually when the lads settled down for the night after warnings from the two guards outside on the small landing.

By morning the four had moved to the far end of the room and were completely ostracized by the rest from that time onward. The tins must have been hidden somewhere while we had covered for them on that extra roll call. This intrigued us, and we intended to locate them.

The answer was supplied by one of the chaps, who was excused duties and confined to the room with a badly swollen ankle, twisted on the rubble. He could speak a little German, and to improve on his vocabulary during his confinement, he got into conversation with a guard stationed inside the factory, who told him various aspects of the Scotsman's activities. Apparently the Scot was always, when possible, hanging around Stossmeister, possibly because Stossmeister spoke reasonable French. What the two of them discussed no one knew. Whatever was said between them, the Scot was always excused work outside the factory, such as rubble clearing. Most of the time he spent on the scrounge inside or outside in the factory grounds. He had a habit of collecting lengths of strong rope, which he told the guard was for binding up wood. It was this fact that gave a clue to the whereabouts of the tins.

Our room had a fifteen to sixteen foot high wooden ceiling with a trap door in the corner that indicated a loft room above. It was unreachable without a ladder, but two three-tiered bunks lashed together then manhandled into position, would allow an agile man to reach and open the trap door. A rope ladder firmly fixed inside the loft would dispense with bunks, and a long pole with a hooked end could manipulate the trap door up and down and the rope ladder hidden, or retrieved for use. Holes and scuff marks on the wooden floor indicated a flight of wooden stairs had given access to the loft.

All that was needed to test our theory was opportunity which meant getting the double-crossing quartet out of the room for enough time to investigate without their knowledge. Meanwhile another query; if a pole had been used on the trap door, where was it hidden? There was no sign of anything suitable in the room and nowhere on the stairs or landing could hide a pole of such length. Furthermore, it would have to be easily accessible for them. If we could find the pole, we had virtually proven our theory.

I was sitting, knees up, back against the wall, gazing abstractly through my dry tea and baccy cigarette smoke at a damp patch of plaster on the opposite wall beside a window I had boarded up after the bombing. Before boarding it up, I had noticed the drain pipe from roof gutter to window sill had been blasted away with the window, hence the damp wall, but the remaining pipe was intact from the window sill downwards. Where better to hide a long, hook ended pole? I nipped out my cigarette, waited about fifteen minutes, then got up and sauntered causally over to a man occupying a bed space by the window, all the time I was studying the boarded up window carefully.

The board showed definite signs of having been tampered

with; small dents, and scratches were quite visible, chips around the edges had been rubbed with dirt to try to conceal them. None of these marks had been there when I first fitted it. I cadged a light for my dog-end from the chap on the floor, sauntered back to where the camp leader was sitting, and nonchalantly gave him my views, adding 'What are we going to do about it?'

'Hold hard,' he replied, 'let's bide our time, we'll get even with the bastards.'

Our chance came on the Friday evening. Having knocked off work early we had a good two and a half hours before roll call. Our group, after making the camp leader aware of our plan, and with his full approval, spread the rumour that we had found a glut of tins of food, again in Magdeburg. The cellar had an easy access and was only about thirty yards from the other cellar which Jock's team had already ransacked. By telling the noted rumour mongers, we knew sure Shifty Jock, and his henchmen would get to know. We added that the bulldozers were in that area, and early the next day the lots were to be levelled.

It was only a matter of about ten minutes when Shifty Jock, the cellar clearer, came over to where we were sitting. He started the same old story, about if we let them know where to go, (we almost told them, go to hell) they would get the hand cart and bring the lot back, and share it out amongst all the other lads. We said, 'What like the last bloody lot?' One of his mates who had accompanied him, butted in, saying, 'No! We realise we made a big mistake over the other tins, and we would like to put things right by getting the tins for the chaps we have let down.' We appeared reluctant to tell them but after shilly-shallying about and some heated words, the camp leader stepped in (as planned) and gave a decision in Jock's favour.

Our trickery was a success and they never stopped to say thanks. I had already been in most of the cellars in that area, prior to them bulldozing it, all of which yielded nought in the way of food. The lookout we had posted saw the four fake Frenchmen pass through the factory gates unquestioned by the guard as in the previous case, pushing the hand cart.

With the thumbs up from our lookout, we set to work on the window using our spoons as levers. The boarding came away easily and it was obvious the nail holes had been eased for quick withdrawal. Six inches or so below the window sill was the end of the broken drainpipe and, sure enough, a bent six inch nail was clearly visible hanging over the end of the pipe. We withdrew the nailed end to find it had been driven into two long broom stales joined together with a length of steel tube making the pole twelve foot long or so. My hunch had paid off.

With a few minutes' practice the pole could be manipulated accurately so we all gathered under the trap door to test another hunch. The pole was applied to the trap door which opened easily, coming to rest against the roof rafters, we then began probing the unhinged sides of the trap's aperture for a rope, but without success. The loft was in pitch darkness, and even a German hand torch, salvaged from the rubble, failed to give sufficient light to see where we were probing. Perhaps something other than a rope ladder had been used? We couldn't use the bunk method to gain access if our lookout gave the warning of an approaching guard, we would have to disperse immediately. Then an idea was put forward. We had so far probed the edge of the aperture. Now, supposing the ladder if existing at all, was hooked higher up in the loft to avoid discovery. We started probing again at different heights and at various angles and then bingo! Our pole man was struck on his shoulder with a small steel ring, attached to the end of a treble stranded rope knotted approximately every eighteen inches along its length.

The two most nimble men amongst us were selected for the ascent and armed with the torch, while two anchor-men steadied the rope, one holding the swinging ring. They disappeared for a few minutes, then one head reappeared, grinning, *'Don't need the torch, there's candles up here, throw some matches up.'* Within a minute, the other chap's face appeared, 'Hold a blanket out down there,' he said in a very excited voice, we did, and amid much scuffling above, tins of food fell fast and furiously. Four chaps held the blanket to start with, but two more had to join the bearers to support the additional weight.

Eventually the two shinned back down the ladder, both smiling contentedly. Our total haul was around two hundred tins, three tins apiece, leaving the remainder to be drawn for later in a free raffle. A dozen tins were left for Shifty Jock and his three stooges, to prove we were not all like them, unwilling to share. Rats like to rummage in empty food tins, we'll teach them rats a lesson, said the camp leader, throwing an empty tin back into the loft. The same attitude was adopted by most of the other prisoners, and within half an hour of share out, at least eighty empty tins had been slung back in the loft. Almost all the chaps succumbed to their hunger, and scoffed one or two tins of food, disregarding whatever they contained. The chaps who could fight off this urge for food, and wished to keep it for later, would have to make their own tins disposal arrangements.

Our rope ladder climbers confirmed the ladder had been firmly tied to a ceiling rafter, and had apparently hung over a hand rail about two foot high at the trap entrance, unseen from the floor below, this accounted for our difficulty in locating it. Demonstrating, one of the loft searchers took the steel ring and cast it in the direction of the rail, at the first attempt the ring rebounded, just missing him. A shout of *watch out!* made him duck, thus avoiding a clout round the head. The loose ring was caught by his mate, and with a second attempt the ladder completely disappeared. We hooked the trap door shut with a slam, replaced the pole in the drain pipe, and refitted the board over the window, then rubbed in dirt over the nail holes and any newly made marks to show it had not been tampered with. Then with the comforting feeling of a full tummy we laid on our blanket pleased and contented. The lucky ones had a smoke, while the remainder just rested and talked.

The four double crossing rats arrived back just after six thirty and went straight to their corner at the far end of the room remaining in huddled conversation till lights out. They

85

obviously thought we had sent them on a wild goose chase for revenge, but they had a bigger surprise awaiting them in the loft. Admittedly, they still had plenty of tins up in the loft, but empty ones, apart from the dozen left for them.

It was a varied conversation on the rubble heaps the next day, but the main item was the Scot and his dilemma. With one of our chaps still confined to the room with his leg injury, this hampered Shifty Jock in his attempt to get at his food cache, and when he did, he'd find the cupboard bare, apart from our discarded tins and the dozen full ones. He would then know why his presence had been required in Magdeburg.

18

Our prime consideration was, as always, food; no food parcels at all were getting through to us now. Our camp leader approached the commandant on our behalf, and broached the topic. The commandant's reply on the subject was, 'Blame your R.A.F. for the shortage of food parcels, they are bombing all our trains, and warehouses. Parcels will be issued, when and if they become available.'

All barter trading was now completely finished, as all cigarettes, or other personal parcels from home had ceased. Scavenging for food was a priority as prison rations had now reached starvation level.

The increasing laxity of our old guard allowed us to roam farther afield. Two could slip away at times, unnoticed. A team mate reported finding a cellar containing piles of potatoes, mostly rotten, and smelling so foul he had to abandon his search and get into the fresh air yet he still had a spasm of vomiting. Being desperate for food, and given the location of the cellar, I decided to try, but also gave up, for although I had dampened the small sack to use as a mask, the stench was still appalling. Disappointed, and with empty pockets, I started picking my way through the heaps of rubble and headed back to the others. Suddenly I remembered the North Sea Fisheries sign I had seen. This started me scrounging around for cellars.

The two or three unsuccessful attempts at what looked like cellar entrances, only depressed me more. Half an hour I must have wasted kicking and rummaging through the rubble and huge mountains of debris, brick, wood, concrete, and iron, hindered my progress. As I walked over an old blown off door, checking first to make sure it was secure, I detected a hollow sound from beneath. Pushing the door aside revealed a cellar entrance and descending the steps cautiously, groping my way with my hands and feet, I came to an abrupt halt, a slab of masonry blocked my advance. The strong smell of fish drove me to try the impossible, but the removal of this obstruction was a two man job.

I retraced my steps and hurried for help, on my arrival I was greeted with, 'Where the hell have you been?' I gave them a quick explanation, then picked the strongest chap from the team and returned full of determination to somehow get into that cellar. Showing my helper the task now before us I sat on a step, my legs slightly bent and both feet placed firmly against the jammed obstruction. My mate armed with a crowbar; a length of thick iron piping found in the rubble, stood a step higher. Pressure was then applied.

The piece of masonry gave suddenly, and tumbled well clear of the bottom step, causing a cloud of dust to engulf us. With the clearing of the dust, the pungent smell of fish, mouldy, and partly burnt potatoes, indicated we were in the basement of North Sea Fisheries.

The very bad light in the basement filtered through the partly blown-in ceiling, making it impossible to define any objects with clarity. As we fumbled around, our hands made contact with a wall of small flat wooden boxes, my mate could stand the stink no more, saying, 'Let's take a box each and get out of this stinking place, into some fresh air.' Outside we opened a box and the smell almost made me sick, we threw both boxes back cursing our luck.

We stood by the cellar entrance a minute or two inhaling the fresh air, then returned to the cellar to try and salvage some edible potatoes, which we luckily found. On our way out I said 'Hold it a minute, I must have a pee.' '*Well don't do it over the potatoes, we may need some more later*,' was his reply.

I made for the nearest corner as my mate ascended the steps to wait for me outside. I was almost at the corner when I stumbled and my groping hand came to rest on what must have been a low shelf. On regaining my balance I found this shelf was stacked with a quantity of oval shaped tins. I forgot about having a pee, at least for the time being, and picked up a tin and shook it. Whatever it contained it sounded solid. I grabbed several tins and made my way to the steps, here the light was good enough for me to see what I had found. On opening a tin, I couldn't believe my luck, my mouth watered as my eyes beheld six large sardines tightly packed in oil. It took only a few seconds to know they were edible. As the first fish dissolved in my mouth, I offered a taster to my mate for his approval, which I received not in words, but in the satisfactory look on his face. Our pockets were emptied of the now unwanted potatoes, and down the cellar we scrambled, emerging some few minutes later with hands full and pockets crammed with tins.

Leaving him to gorge himself, I ducked behind a heap of rubble and had my long awaited pee. Between mouthfuls of sardines he made his way back to the other chaps, I arrived, as he was throwing tins to our mates, telling them to dig in, we have plenty.

This boost to our daily ration was a godsend, but wishing no repetition of the last food episode, we refrained from taking any of the tins back to the factory. The other rubble parties were obviously doing the same as us, with varying degrees of success, and obviously keeping their successes a secret. Before leaving the site, I slipped back and camouflaged the cellar entrance, by using the old door and throwing a few shovelfuls of rubble on top.

19

The Allied troops were now within a few miles of Magdeburg, and we could hear their artillery in the distance, which led to rumours that we were going to be moved to another camp farther inland. This seemed confirmed when we were told there would be no further work parties and we were confined to our room. With the build up of activity, and the strong troop reinforcements around the outskirts of the town our move seemed inevitable. This change in routine forced the Scotsman to approach our camp leader to tell him what I had recently suspected, namely, that he was not going to move to another camp but would remain hidden in the loft with his three mates until the Allies arrived. An unwritten law in any P.O.W. camp was to assist any person attempting an escape if possible and this move by Jock and Co. would be classified as escaping. In spite of our feelings towards the four scurrilous characters, our camp leader nodded his approval. To the Scot's bemusement we removed the window board, retrieved the pole, opened the trap and hooked down the ladder. The four stood eyeing us sheepishly and suspecting the worst. No good luck or words of cheer were exchanged as we stood watching the first man up hoist their gear into the loft followed by the other three. They closed the trap behind them. We replaced the pole, then the window board, and waited for orders to move out.

Some ten minutes later we were ordered downstairs and assembled in front of the factory, and without having a roll call or search (which saved us covering for at least four missing prisoners), we headed through the gate. The road was full of German soldiers, and armoured units, all heading towards Magdeburg, behind them, a contingent of the Hitler Youth, some as young as ten or eleven. On both sides of the road other units of the Hitler Youth were entrenched at intervals, all dressed in seemingly new uniforms, and armed with various weapons, mostly anti-tank guns. Many of the little buggers spat and swore at us, as we waited for more military vehicles to pass. The abuse ceased, when a German officer yelled orders to them, although we were still a target for their spittle.

We finally moved out in the opposite direction, heading towards the river Elbe. We had been walking about two hours when we came to a bridge across the river, we also came to an abrupt halt. There was a hell of a lot of confusion all around the bridge area, it was bedlam; womenfolk shouting at their children, men cursed and swore about how long they had been waiting, and officers repeatedly yelled orders to the army personnel. The entire bridge was a seething mass of civilian refugees, pushing prams, bicycles, and pushcarts laden with young, whimpering children perched on the families' belongings, all moving (or trying to) in the same direction. This, with the long formations of German soldiers trying to pass in the opposite direction, resulted in absolute chaos.

We sat by the roadside and waited for about half an hour, during which time a meagre bread ration was dished out, but the situation did not improve, it deteriorated if anything, and eventually our officer ordered us to our feet.

Leaving the bridge, we started along the road running parallel with the river, which gradually veered away and soon we were in narrow country lanes, and passing through small hamlets. Most of these were now uninhabited, apart from a very few old people, and a stray dog or two.

By the time the next village was reached it was too dark to continue further, and we were told to use a large derelict barn by the wayside to sleep in. Dog tired, we threw ourselves into the hay to sleep, but our rest was short lived. I suddenly felt something moving slowly around my neck, and instantly I grabbed suspiciously at my throat, trapping a large rat, which I hurled violently against the barn's wooden wall, there was a dull thud, a horrible squeal; its death was instantaneous. A few moments later, I felt my overcoat pocket moving, inside was another rat happily eating my small bread ration. Dropping the coat to the ground, I quickly stamped it underfoot, and after removing the dead vermin, I decided to finish off the remaining bread myself, as soon as it was light enough to see what I was eating. I noticed some other fellows who still had their bread ration left, intended doing the same thing, as the rats were everywhere; the whole barn was infested with them. Almost all of us ended up outside sitting with our backs to the barn wall, in the very cold night air, dozing off only occasionally till daybreak, which everyone was glad to see. I was hungry as usual, so I ate the remains of my bread ration, including the crumbs unwanted by the rat. An hour or so later we were given some ersatz coffee, then we were on the move again.

We did not know where we were going, I'm sure our guards themselves were in the dark as to our destination, they just followed the chap in front. Somehow we seemed to be heading in the direction of the river again, and about an hour later it came into sight, also another bridge, the latter being obscured by a clump of trees. As we approached we could see the bridge clearly. Apparently, orders had been given for the bridge to be destroyed and a team of sappers hung from its structure were placing charges and the bridge was now closed to all pedestrian and vehicle traffic.

Seeing the predicament, a short rest was ordered to allow the officer to consult his map, and to issue new orders, then we resumed our march. Within a few hundred yards we noticed the river again veering away to our left, then suddenly it vanished completely. We were now passing more refugees moving in the opposite direction, most of them on foot, although there were quite a fair number of cars and lorries, all of which were laden to the roof with belongings. Our slight pause for only that few minutes seemed to have eased some of the refugees' problem, and apart from groups of stragglers, most of which were elderly people with young helpers, and a dog or two, our path ahead was clear. We never stopped again until early evening, when we were given a mess tin half-full of almost cold coffee, and another meagre ration of bread, which after last night's experience with the rats, I ate immediately.

That night we slept under an old Dutch barn, a slight smell of burnt straw and charred wood still lingered, giving us the impression that the fire had been recent. I stirred after what had, to me, seemed only an hour or so, to find a new day had begun.

Although we had all been awoken early, our officer showed no urgency in moving us out, and we had to hang about for well over two hours, before we finally had orders to move off. By noon, after only travelling a few miles, we entered a small village, on the outskirts of which was a signpost with largish black lettering, partly obscured by a low overgrown hedgerow. To me, I thought the sign gave the name of the village as 'Colbitz' (not to be confused with the infamous 'Colditz'). I could have been mistaken, but if I had read that sign correctly, we had not travelled very far from Magdeburg. I had had the impression for quite some time, that we had been walking around in circles most of the time.

As we moved right into the village, we came face to face with another large group of British P.O.W.s, how many would be hard to say, at least a hundred and fifty, they were guarded it seemed more by German officers than the ordinary run-of-the-mill soldier. We were kept separate from the other group of prisoners, who seemed to have been on the march for some considerable time, our group were tired, hungry, and downhearted, but we looked at them pityingly. Our officer gathered us around him in a little field, in the distance we could hear the noises of war, and realized the Allied troops were near at hand. The officer addressed us,

'This village is in a neutral zone. All advancing combatant troops have been notified not to shell or bomb this area, as only British prisoners of war and their guards, are temporarily stationed in this village. No resistance or offensive action will be taken against any advancing troops, either by the military or civilian population. To show we are only thinking of your safety and well-being, we have dispatched a senior German officer who is now trying to contact any of our enemies' forward troops, to implement the surrender of this village. In your own interests stay together, and remain where you are until this occurs.'

A huge sigh of relief spread through us, and we found ourselves cheerfully laughing and slapping each other on the backs. Some of the longer termed prisoners were even moved to tears. Two hours elapsed without any sign of the mediating officers return. What happened to this venture no one seemed to know, we waited patiently, but discontent was running high amongst the prisoners. The continuous unrest forced the German officer again, to send another mediator on the same mission, this time, the German officer and a guard, both unarmed, were accompanied by two British prisoners. They returned about an hour later, both the P.O.W.s, seemed very happy and poked their thumbs up as they passed us. The word soon got around that contact had been made, and negotiations were settled. Waiting was now more tolerable.

Within the hour we could hear the rumble of tanks approaching and intermittent small arms fire. Whatever army it was advancing on the village we did not know, it could have been the Germans. Ignoring the officer's warning to stay put we ran to the outskirts of the village as a large Yankee tank appeared and ground to a halt a few yards from us. Behind it was a convoy of lorries carrying American troops, everyone was shouting, cheering and offering outstretched hands. The sight of these troops had a strange emotional effect on us more than some prisoners could endure; tears of joy trickled down their faces. As we walked the length of the convoy, cartons of cigarettes, not packets, were being passed down to us along with Yankee combat food packages, or, as they called them, 'K' rations. Unable to remember the date of this liberation day, my curiosity became aroused, so I asked a Yank, it was Friday the Thirteenth.

We must have presented a nondescript sight to these Yanks, few of us had a full British uniform, the bits we did have were made up from British, French, Italian, and a few wore American trousers. We had spoken to the American soldiers for about half an hour, then the tank and a few lorries moved off skirting the village. Just as they were slowly moving away, one of the drivers said, 'You speak very good English, do you mind telling me what is your nationality?' A little Londoner shouted, 'I'm a blinking Cockney, I am.' The reason they couldn't identify us as British, apart from our poor uniforms, and the fact we had not washed or shaved for over three days, could have been put down to our very bad English. We spoke camp jargon. This, although mostly English, was derived from a smattering of German, Italian, French, and a bit of Hindustani, picked up in various camps.

Other American tanks had moved up and were now rumbling into the village centre, where the entire German garrison had assembled in formation, their weaponry stacked in rows on the ground before them. The German officers, stood approximately six paces in front of the other ranks, at an arm's length interval, with their senior officer in front of the whole company, all stood smartly at attention. As we watched this procedure a Jeep drew up, and three American officers jumped out and approached the German commandant, to formally accept the surrender of the village.

Prior to this official hand-over, our German camp commandant had handed his Luger pistol to our English camp leader with the request to be shot. Refusing his invitation, and asking why, the commandant said, 'I do not wish to be subject to the atrocities which I have been told happen to German officers in Allied P.O.W. camps; beatings, starvation, and torture. It would be better to be dead.' Ignoring the slanderous talk, our camp leader returned the unloaded pistol to him, with just one comment; 'Bullshit.'

20

A large barn was used to search and briefly question the officers, who would be interrogated thoroughly on the arrival at American headquarters; the other ranks, were lined up almost where they stood to be searched. I suppose it was vindictive pleasure, but we could not resist watching the German soldiers being searched by the Yanks. The searching was so casual and pathetic, hardly a thing was taken from them, pen-knives, razors, lighters, and matches, all remained in their possession. Remembering the articles stolen from us, cigarette cases, rings, watches, including all foregoing articles, had all been shared and pocketed by our captors. This started our chaps complaining to the sergeant in charge. 'Why don't you search the bastards thoroughly? The way the thieving sods searched us.' To which the sergeant replied, 'Why don't you search them yourselves?'

We did. It was not a strip-off search, but we gave them a bloody good going over, and all those Germans ended up with was personal papers, photographs, letters from home etc. Amid shouts of dismay and protests, the now Kriegsgefangene (P.O.W.), watched helplessly at the ever growing heap of confiscated items on the ground. The Yankee sergeant who had witnessed the keenness of our search, thought it too vindictive and harsh, and let them have their cigarettes, tobacco, lighters, and matches back.

On completing our search, the prisoners were hustled onto lorries, and made to stand packed like sardines, all the way to their internment. The last lorry being so full, one little chubby Unteroffizer had twice tried to climb on, at his third attempt, his posterior was hanging over the tailboard, his trousers had pulled very tight across his fat bum. The driver had found a long broad-bladed sword and was getting very impatient, viciously he brought the flat of the blade whipping across the

Unteroffizer's backside, yelling, 'Get on there you bloody Kraut.' Like lightning, and amid shouts of protest from those already aboard, he landed higgledy-piggledy amongst his fellow prisoners, causing more confusion. The Yank looked at us, laughed, then said, 'That moved the fat bastard.' He threw the sword in his cab, jumped in himself, and seconds later, jamming his foot hard on the accelerator, he drove his tumbling passengers away. We sat and waited, as ordered by an American officer, for our transport to arrive. This time we spent stuffing Yankee 'K' rations, and smoking Yankee cigarettes. Life seemed more pleasant now than it had for months.

Eventually a convoy of empty lorries rigged with bench seats arrived. I finished up on the last lorry with five other chaps. We sat three on each side, and were driven away in reasonable comfort. I don't know if it was my imagination, but to me that lorry appeared to have had a jinx on it. We had only travelled a few miles when one of the back tyres punctured. We stopped, after a quick check by kicking it, our driver shouted, 'It's okay only a flat.'

We continued for about thirty miles, this distance was soon covered, as the driver had his foot down, trying to catch up with the convoy who had left us well behind while we had stopped to examine the puncture.

Our journey was mostly through open countryside and small villages, we did go through one big town, where it seemed only the main road was passable. The town was just heaps of rubble, and completely deserted, not even a scavenging dog could be seen; it was a ghost town. The back wheel by now had heated up so much, and the smell of burning rubber was so acrid, another check revealed the second back tyre had punctured, this made us reduce speed considerably. We had only travelled some two miles further when the jinx struck again, another puncture, this time in the front left tyre. It was impossible to change the wheel, as we had previously asked the driver about the vehicle's spare wheels, to which he had replied nonchalantly, '*Lost the darned things buddy.*'

It was now getting dark and the driver decided to crawl along at a walking pace, hoping to reach somewhere to stay for the night. We were in the middle of nowhere, then the outline of a building could be seen some hundred and fifty yards away, this seemed the only sign of habitation. Coming to a halt, our driver dismounted to investigate, it appeared this was a small disused school-house on the outskirts of a deserted village. A middle-aged couple were still in residence, most probably the caretaker and his wife. Between our driver and us, and with much sign language, we managed to explain we were going to shelter there for the night. They showed us into a little classroom where we could bed down. After a 'K' ration supper, we settled down on the wooden tiled floor. Every chance our driver had, he would pester us about P.O.W. life, and our experiences, so before we fell asleep, to satisfy his curiosity, we told him a few tales about prison life. We slept well that night, being so used to sleeping on floor boards, but our Yankee friend, who had never slept rough before, had an uncomfortable, cold, miserable, restless night. Perhaps our stories had given him nightmares.

We were awoken by the driver about 7 am. He had already brewed some coffee, and what a lovely change from that ersatz piddle, this went down well with the breakfast knocked up from 'K' rations, followed by a cigarette. I nipped through to have a sluice under the kitchen tap, sitting there were the middle-aged couple. I only knew a few words of German, but from their conversation I gathered they spoke about the war. The woman said something, which to me was double-Dutch. The man gently placed his hand on her shoulder replying, 'The war is almost over, and Germany is finished.' I thought 'It's about time the German people woke up and realized, all that propaganda about the victorious German forces winning great battles, and in complete control of the war, was just a pack of deceitful lies!'

A short debate between us, and the driver, ended with our driver deciding we would continue crawling along with the lorry, in the hope of meeting someone on the way who could help. We had hardly set forth when an American army lorry approached us from the opposite direction. Our driver flagged him down, and learnt there was an American workshop just a

98

mile further on. This short journey seemed forever, but finally we limped into the workshop and dismounted, leaving a repair team to work on the lorry, which was serviceable within half an hour. Of course, as soon as the repair team found out we were ex P.O.W.s, (thanks to our Yankee friend) the cigarettes and coffee both flowed freely but so did the tiresome questions. The duty officer then had a quick conversation with our driver, pointed out a new map reference and we were on our way again. What a marvellous relief to get away from the inquisitive, question-firing Yanks, who would have had us there all day, reminiscing. Apart from another relief, the call of nature, we travelled non stop for about an hour until we reached our destination, an American evacuation hospital.

21

The hospital was in a large grassy field and under canvas, six large marquees, with a dozen or so smaller marquees surrounding them, all spick and span, and neatly signposted. We were taken to one of the large marquees which was a dining area, with a cookhouse at the rear, and told we could have as much food as we wished, and whatever we wished, providing it was on the menu. I wasn't particularly hungry at that moment, as I had eaten well on 'K' rations prior to leaving the village school. I settled for a couple of soft boiled eggs, white bread and butter, toast and marmalade, with two big mugs of tea; food I had only dreamt about over the past months. As we ate, more lorries arrived, and the marquee began to fill up with more ex P.O.W.s, and was almost full by the time we had finished.

Some of the late-comers had suffered much more than others, some limping, others frail tired wretches held up by mates for support. The cookhouse staff were very busy, they were working at full capacity, with long queues still waiting to be catered for.

Some prisoners, boasted they could eat a whole chicken, and to their amazement were given a small chicken, with the rest of their tray piled high with roast and creamed potatoes, and mixed vegetables. As we left the dining tent they were wolfing it down like starving dogs.

We followed an officer who took us to another smaller marquee which was one of the hospital wards, this contained four rows of white sheeted beds stretching its length with a latrine and ablutions room annex at the back. You can select any bed you wish, we were told, and advised to have an early night and try to get some sleep, as we would be starting on our way home sometime tomorrow. As an afterthought the officer added, 'If anybody feels hungry, or wishes a beverage,

100

there are always cooks on duty, and you can be served at any time.'

I selected a bed, threw my Italian army overcoat on it, then made my way to the ablutions and had a decent wash, the first proper wash for almost a week. It was getting late afternoon when I got back to my bed, the other diners we had left feeding were beginning to drift into the ward, and many headed straight for the latrines to be violently sick. After months of activity on a starvation diet, our stomachs couldn't accept the vast amount of rich food they had just crammed down. Realizing their mistake, warned me to go careful on the food, so I had a late tea, and selected light non greasy foods in minimal quantities, a few others followed my example. With the food being so abundant, and varied, it was very hard to resist the temptation to over-feed.

I decided to turn in for the night, relishing the thought of a lovely soft bed for a change. I slid between the inviting white sheets. I turned one way then the other, I couldn't get to sleep, it was a discomfort lying there. Discouraged and tired, I took a blanket from the bed, folded it, and placed it on the ground next to the bed, threw a pillow to one end, pulled another blanket off to cover myself, within a few minutes I was fast asleep.

I was awoken by the sound of voices, some medical officers stood backs towards me, one saying, 'If I had not seen this for myself I would never have believed it.' They then walked off with their hands behind their backs, still in deep conversation. Getting up I noticed almost every chap had followed my idea, as like our stomachs, our bodies could not adjust to different conditions overnight. I wondered for some days if mine ever would.

Getting up early, gave me a chance to get to the ablutions and have a wash before the rush began. On my return I sat on my bed and had a smoke, by now a few other chaps had washed and were ready, so we trooped down to the dining tent. I just had two poached eggs on toast, and a slice of toast and marmalade, followed by two cups of tea. The cook had tried to tempt me, as he had the others, with a large

101

plate of fried eggs, bacon, sausage, and chips, with as many slices of fried bread, one wished to have, but I declined the offer. Many accepted the cook's tempting breakfast, and many had upset stomachs within the next hour or so.

I sat talking and smoking in the dining tent for the next hour, then accompanied by two other fellows, wandered aimlessly around the hospital field, occasionally meeting other ex P.O.W.s, whose main conversation and thoughts dwelt on home. Just as we returned to our ward, a convoy of empty lorries appeared outside, an officer entered the ward and called us together, 'Okay men, we are going to try to fly you guys home, so if you get aboard the lorries we'll get started.'

I was among the first aboard, our lorry headed the small convoy travelling to the air field, but we did not reach it. As we moved into the approach road, we were stopped by military police who spoke to our driver first, then to us. 'Sorry fellows, we're so jam packed with ex P.O.W.s, we can't accept any more, maybe tomorrow. Meanwhile, the only temporary place to house you is a nearby disused prison camp, sorry we had to resort to such a place. At the very first opportunity you'll be notified when a plane is available. Don't worry, everything has been laid on for you.' Our lorry turned around, stopped, and waited for the others to do the same, then the unhappy convoy moved off. We travelled approximately two miles before reaching the camp.

The rows of familiar huts stood unmistakable beneath the clouding sky, making an uninviting sight, but this depressing view faded when seeing all watch towers and barbed wire had been removed, and not a German uniform in sight. I grinned ruefully when I noticed the old wooden type bunks in all the huts, had been replaced with white sheeted single beds, realizing nobody would ever use the bunks again as Allied P.O.W.s. One of the largest huts had been turned into a dining room-cum-cookhouse, and the quality and quantity of the food was as lavish as ever. The camp, we were told was on the outskirts of a town named Dorsten, which apparently was out of bounds to all service men, meaning us mostly. I had another enjoyable well chosen meal, after which, a few other chaps and I decided to take a stroll around the boundary of the camp, now defined by wire free poles, spaced at irregular intervals some had vanished, possibly for fire wood. We had been warned not to stray too far, in case there was a sudden recall to the airfield.

It was while on our stroll, for the first time, the full impact of my new found freedom struck me, and I felt a strange elation I had never experienced before. Delayed action, maybe, but I had a strong urge to shout out loud, which perhaps I did, as one chap said, 'Don't it make a bloody good change to look at a prisoner of war camp, from the other side of the wire.'

The anticipation of going home spoilt everybody's sleep that night, and the mess hall was full at an early hour, with men all hoping this would be their last day in Germany. During the meal, we were told that another attempt would be made to get us away, and our transport arrived within the hour. We entered the airfield and dismounted, then we were taken to a bench filled hangar, where we sat smoking and drinking tea, like hundreds of others. After a day's wait, and an abundance of apologies, fresh lorries returned us to the P.O.W. camp, with a promise of a definite flight out next day. This became a repeat performance for the next two days, by which time the whole camp was becoming browned off, and disheartened, although we knew the Yanks were doing everything they could to get us home.

By now this temporary camp had swollen in numbers, our original group of fifty-nine, had multiplied to well over the six hundred mark. It was good to know that the Americans worked to a very strict rota, especially concerning us ex-prisoners, with our group being the first on the list from that camp.

On the third day back we went to the airfield, this was getting monotonous, but this time we never went to the hangar but joined a throng of other ex P.O.W.s, and were separated into groups of a hundred men, and told to wait our turn beside the runway. Our group was placed third in priority order, an excellent position for us, as some three thousand ex-prisoners waited hopefully. The incoming planes were mostly Dakotas, which were landing and taking off at irregular intervals, unfortunately not all the incoming planes loaded up with ex-prisoners, although a majority did, and our queue was getting shorter with every plane load. At last, after hours of patiently waiting, I thought, the next plane, I'll be okay for that one, and at approximately 4.30pm, our turn came.

A Dakota taxied to a stop near our group, and a Yankee sergeant beckoned us forward, 'Okay you guys, keep a-coming.' And as each man boarded he handed them a brown paper bag, saying, 'You may need this, it can get damned bumpy up there,' pointing his gloved thumb skywards. It was only by the skin of my teeth that I made it, I was the last one allowed to board, and I knew how those left behind felt, when the sergeant said, 'Sorry chaps, that's the lot for this trip.' The door slammed shut, then the plane moved off in a wide arc to face the runway, the minutes, which seemed like an hour, ticked by, then we were airborne.

In those few waiting minutes, I had noticed another twenty lorries unloading more ex-prisoners, none of which would be lucky enough to get away that day, but perhaps in three or four days' time if our past experiences were anything to go by. About five minutes after take off an American liaison officer, who was escorting us on the journey, told us we would be landing at Brussels to await transport by British planes to England. We were on our way home at last, but not direct to England, as everyone had hoped.

22

We touched down just outside Brussels, and were taken by awaiting lorries to a large hostel, run by the NAAFI. On arrival, each man was given a cardboard box, containing cigarettes, chocolate, and toilet articles, then taken to the dining room and served with a hot appetizing meal. This, although not so varied, had been prepared by British personnel, and had been planned to cater for the returning starving ex-prisoners. Later, after the meal and a smoke, we joined other new arrivals, and the entire group were taken to a largish bed-filled room, our accommodation for the night.

In the morning while having breakfast, an English army major entered the dining room, calling for attention said, 'You are free to do as you wish today. No transport can be supplied unfortunately, so if you go out, make sure you're back here at sixteen hundred hours. With luck, we may be able to fly you home this evening.'

The thoughts of home induced more chatter to fill the room, and eventually to gain a little peace, four of us left for a walk into Brussels. We roamed around for a few hours, not one of us had a penny piece in our pockets, as no currency had been granted to any returning prisoners, so getting fed up, we headed back to the hostel. We had arrived back too early for tea, but cups of tea were usually available, so we sat drinking tea, and smoking in a small ante-room. It was about 4.15pm when our chatter was interrupted by an officer. He asked us to assemble in the dining room where an army captain told us to collect our belongings, and board the awaiting lorries. Within a matter of minutes, the convoy was pulling away, heading towards the airfield.

Our arrival at the airfield triggered off thoughts of our previous attempts of being airlifted home, the only planes parked around the apron of the field, were a few private aircraft. '*If they are going to use them,*' someone said, '*it'll take them bloody weeks to get us home!*'

On our right, but concealed from view by a hangar, was another operational runway. As we approached a Lancaster bomber was ticking over and already men were getting aboard, but I missed my chance on that by just two passengers.

The next thirty minutes as we waited for another plane to taxi in passed monotonously. The slight drizzle only added to our misery, making our waiting seem like eternity. Another Lancaster bomber circled the field, then landed and taxied towards us. As it stopped rolling the order was given and I was among the first to go aboard. I was told by the pilot to move to the extreme front of the plane. Two of us finished up in a small compartment partly surrounded by perspex windows. It took about ten minutes for our plane to load up, then within minutes of the last man getting aboard, we were airborne.

Being so glad to be homeward bound, the speed or height of our flight never interested me, but during the flight, something about seven thousand feet was mentioned in a conversation between the navigator and the pilot. As far as I was concerned, they could have been talking about anything; my mind was on other matters.

It was almost dusk when we came in to land at a place called Westcott. Awaiting lorries took us from the airfield to a nearby army barracks. Here a sergeant-major, bespectacled, and sporting a military moustache, took us to the cookhouse for our first meal on British soil. With the meal over, we had time to have a cigarette, then we were taken to have a shower, and shown the Nissen hut we were to sleep in.

Everyone had a sleepless night apart from the cook who could have overslept as breakfast was very late. We had all washed and shaved and sat on our beds in the Nissen hut smoking for a couple of hours. This may have been arranged to keep us separated from the young rookies we had noticed while we awaited breakfast. I could not see any sense in this, but that's the army.

106

With breakfast over, we reported to another Nissen hut containing rows of trestle tables, and were told to get a chair from the stack and find a place behind them while a corporal issued us each with a printed sheet of paper and a pen. An appropriate heading for these sheets could have been 'Questionnaire for Returning British Ex-prisoners of War' for that was their function. A blank sheet of paper was attached for additional information.

An officer entered, dismissed the corporal, and addressed us. 'You will find ink on the tables. Now, every question on your sheets must be answered, put your finished papers on the small table by the door. When this is done, and the papers checked, you will be taken to be issued with new uniforms, ration cards, and travelling warrants, etc.'

Apart from name, rank, and number, the sheets required a complete and detailed history of events, including all prison camp names, numbers, dates interned within, campaigns of war prior to capture, any acts of sabotage committed, if so full information of such, and any other relevant information from the day of capture until day of release.

These questions made us meditate: Jerry never told us the dates we moved from camp to camp, which could be three or four camps in as many months. We had been in prison camps, where one day is almost the same as any other, where weeks seem like months, and months seem never-ending. We had no calendars hanging on the walls, denoting high-days and holidays. Half an hour passed in silence, some chaps like myself, had managed to make a few rough notes of the various camps in which we had been interned, finished our papers fairly quickly, and put them on the small table. We returned to our seats and waited patiently in the hushed room, for the remainder to complete their forms. One chap getting irritated and annoyed by so many questions, looked at the officer and yelled, 'These buggers want to know a hell of a lot more about us than the bloody Germans did.' He threw his pen on the table in disgust, what with the delay in not sending us home on leave, and now all these questions, he could not stand it any longer. He blurted out, 'All this bloody red tape, surely it's all unnecessary, after four and a half years in blinking prison camps, I think we are entitled to some consideration.' *'Hear! Hear!'* echoed throughout the hut.

It was well into the afternoon before everyone had finished the question papers, having to stop for dinner, which like the breakfast, was very late. The time just flew by; it was 5.30pm, according to the wall clock in the hut, before all the infernal papers had been sorted and examined. We had tea, which was hurried by all, as nobody really wanted it, getting home was all that interested us, but this had been stipulated in Daily Orders, all ex-prisoners will attend tea parade, with no exemptions. Eventually the officers' promises became facts, we were taken to the quartermaster's stores, and issued with new battle dresses, and other garments. The officer, after satisfying himself that our uniforms fitted us correctly, issued us out ration cards, travel warrants, and other necessary documents, and informed us, other ration cards, and army pay books (A.B.64) will be posted on to us. All this documentation, took up precious time, also became very tedious, finally we were allowed to board the waiting lorries, which took us to the nearest railway station. This was it, the journey dreamt of over the long deprived months of incarceration, it was one of the most happy experiences to befall any returning ex-prisoner of war.

Being late in the day, the station was almost deserted. Small groups made for the various platforms to wait eagerly for their train to arrive. Lucky for some, their train was already in, but in our case, fate had decided otherwise. Having to wait for our train, which seemed would never come, then having to change trains, again another tiresome wait, waiting those dragging minutes seemed like hours, on both occasions. At London our little party split up, as most of them lived in the southern area of England, only two of us caught the same northbound train.

However, luckily for me, my stop was only thirty miles up the line. My temporary travelling companion had, he told me, at least another two hours' journey after my stop. The train at last stopped at my destination, as I handed my travel warrant to the sleepy R.T.O. (Railway Transport Officer), the town hall clock was just striking the last few chimes of midnight. I passed through a familiar station turnstile, and over a familiar foot bridge that led to familiar streets. The name of that place was home. Although not quite, my final destination, was a small slate roofed terrace house some twenty minutes' walk away, at the far end of town. The thought of this, and the reunion with my family boosted my eagerness.

As I walked briskly through the now sleeping town, two Redcaps appeared from nowhere, I approached them cheerfully. 'Hey!' said one, stopping me in my tracks, 'Where do you think you're going at this time of the morning?' If I had spoken my mind, I would have been run in, but I replied in a civil manner. 'Where's your pass?' This I handed him willingly, seeing the words 'Repatriation Leave' boldly stamped across my pass, he instantly demanded to see my pay book. When this was not produced his mate stepped forward and began to question me. From my various papers, I handed him an explanatory document which informed whoever it may concern that I was a released prisoner of war and permitted to be absent from my unit for an indefinite period. Finding he had no lawful reason to detain me, he grudgingly handed back my documents, saying, 'Sorry mate, just doing my job.' I never replied in any way to his comment, but walked off leaving them both standing, it seemed, in deep thought. As I turned to enter the road in which I lived, I could see both the Redcaps staring in my direction, presumably at me. Why they should do so, I could not see any reason, there was no difference between me, an ex-prisoner of war, and any other British soldier, apart from looking haggard and underweight, and on repatriation leave. Admittedly, in all probability, thousands of other British soldiers were home on leave, perhaps embarkation leave, as the war was not yet over. If I still had that K.G. and red triangle painted on my back, I would expect some strange looks. I know if the Redcaps had called me back, I would have ignored them.

Reaching the front door, I lifted the knocker and tapped

lightly. This started our old dog Paddy barking. A minute or so later, a shaft of light from the open bedroom window, broke the darkness, luckily, there were no air raid wardens about, although now, at this late stage of hostilities, the wardens turned a blind eye to a slight infringement of the blackout restrictions. My father's head poked through the window, looking up, with tearful eyes, I said, 'Hello dad.' I heard my mother's sleepy voice say, 'What's the matter, father?' That was the moment I could not hold back my pent up feelings, overwhelmed by emotion, the tears of joy rolled down my flushed cheeks.

Prisoners of War

Barren wastes of scrub and sand,
Dry unfertile desert land,
With barbed wire on every hand,
    Prisoners of war

A helpless host of hungry men,
Crowded like rats in cage and pen,
Shut off, it seems, from human ken,
    Prisoners of war

Ill clad, unkempt and underfed,
Trading their watches and rings for bread,
A chill and concrete floor their bed,
    Prisoners of war

Queuing for hours in blistering heat,
Receiving a morsel of bread and meat,
Glad of even scraps to eat,
    Prisoners of war

Bullied and driven like flocks of sheep,
Treated like dirt from dawn to sleep,
Hearts being filled with hatred deep,
    Prisoners of war

Shut off from news of the outside world,
Sifting the truth from the truths that are hurled,
Silently keeping the flag unfurled,
    Prisoners of war

Striving to keep alive your hope,
Feeling at times it's beyond your scope,
Drugging yourself with rumours as dope,
    Prisoners of war

Setting new value on trivial things,
The smell of the flowers, the skylark that sings,
The beauty and grace of a butterfly's wings,
	Prisoners of war

Learning that life without freedom is vain,
'Tis better to die than live ever in pain,
Thank God for some hope of release once again,
	Prisoners of war

Seeing new meanings in higher things,
In life in Christ, in the hopes he brings,
Thus did they treat the king of kings,
	Prisoners of war

Finding at last if you've eyes to see,
This glorious truth fixed by God's decree,
As long as the soul is unchained, you're free,
	Prisoners of war

					anon

I first read this poem in Stalag IIa, it was handed to me by a
fellow prisoner. The grubby, well handled paper was barely
legible. I therefore apologize to the poet, for any incorrect
wording.